BULLET PROOF

The Safe and Secure
Retirement Income Plan

BRAD PISTOLE

Bullet Proof

Copyright © 2021 Brad Pistole

All rights reserved.

No portion of this book may be reproduced mechanically, electronically, or by any other means, including photocopying, without written permission of the author. It is illegal to copy the book, post it to a website, or distribute it by any other means without permission from the author.

Disclaimer

This publication is designed to provide accurate and authoritative information regarding the subject matter contained within. It should be understood that the author and publisher are not engaged in rendering legal, accounting, or other financial service through this medium. The author and publisher shall not be liable for your misuse of this material and shall have neither liability nor responsibility to anyone with respect to any loss or damage caused or alleged to be caused, directly or indirectly, by the information contained in this book. The author and/or publisher do not guarantee that anyone following these strategies, suggestions, tips, ideas, or techniques will become successful. If legal advice or other expert assistance is required, the services of a competent professional should be sought.

www.ExpertPress.net

Table of Contents

Client Testimonials 5
Dedication 9
Acknowledgments 11
Foreword 13
Introduction 19

Chapter 1
Houston, We Have a Problem 27

Chapter 2
Pressing Your Luck 39

Chapter 3
Taking Inventory 51

Chapter 4
Laying the Right Foundation 63

Chapter 5
Choosing the Right Retirement Vehicle for Your Family 79

Chapter 6
Guaranteed Lifetime Income 101

Chapter 7
Guaranteed "Tax-Free" Lifetime Income (Even Better) 119

Chapter 8
Pursuing What Matters Most 131

Choosing the Right Financial Team 145

About the Author 153

Client Testimonials

In 2019, my wife, Judy, and I listened to Brad's radio show and felt prompted to make an appointment with him to find out more about protecting our money in retirement. We are so glad we did! With the expertise he provided, we've already taken some important steps to protect our retirement assets. Brad does a wonderful job of teaching about retirement, explaining options, and answering questions. What surprised us about Brad was his willingness to spend time with us, always making sure that we understood the different products and were comfortable moving forward. We find him to be a person with great knowledge, good character, and totally trustworthy.

—Scott McChrystal
CH (COL), USA (Retired)
Military Rep and Endorser
Assemblies of God Chaplaincy Ministries
Springfield, Missouri

Since first meeting Brad, we have been more impressed by his financial knowledge than by any other financial advisor we have ever met. We are also impressed with his thoroughness in presenting the benefits of annuities. We feel he goes out of his way to take care of us as clients, and one of the main things we like is his prompt manner of keeping appointments. We had been in the market 100 percent for many years, but now, at our ages and with the uncertainty of the market, we feel much more at ease with what Brad has taught us about protecting our assets. We would urge anyone to sit down with Brad to let him show you the tools he uses to ensure the safety of your funds. We trust him implicitly and feel very secure with the programs he represents. Brad is the most efficient, pleasant, and knowledgeable person we have ever dealt with in the financial arena.

—Hugh and Clara Kirkland
Springfield, Missouri

In 2010, I would listen to Safe Money Radio as I returned home from church on Sunday mornings. After several weeks, I knew I needed more information about this financial plan that sounded too good to be true. The first meeting with Brad exceeded all expectations. His honesty and integrity were evident. I have placed my trust and confidence in Brad as he has taught me and guided me down a secure financial pathway. He has not let me down. I just wish I had learned about Brad and Safe Money Radio two years earlier (when 2008 happened!).

—*Phyllis Fennell*
Nixa, Missouri

My wife and I responded to Brad's invitation to attend his financial planning seminar, where he presented profound information on fixed indexed annuities. It was an excellent presentation that evening. We wanted to get out of the market, especially my wife, because of the risks involved. We moved here from California and began looking for a local investor. We met with Brad at least four times, where he graciously gave his time answering all of our concerns. After feeling confident with him, we moved a substantial amount of money from the market to a fixed indexed annuity. As we are in our seventies, we feel comfortable with the decision, and my wife has had the best nights' sleep in a long time. We are also pleased after spending time with Brad to know that he operates a faith-based business.

—*Jim and Ruth Roberts*
Ozark, Missouri

With the uncertain financial market, I had been looking for a more stable financial base to diversify some of my holdings. I first heard Brad on the local radio station and was so impressed that I ordered his package of information by mail. After reading his book and materials, I called Brad, and my wife and I met with him. I was so impressed that I called my brother and asked him to go back with me to meet Brad. His programs have given both of our families a sense of peace and less stress. Brad is always available and returns our calls promptly. His knowledge of IRAs and financial programs and his honesty and faith make him not only our advisor but someone we are proud to call a friend.

—James Y. Fairbairn
Springfield, Missouri

Dedication

This book is dedicated to my best friend, Kimberley Grace. Thank you for all your hard work editing my follow-up to Safe Money Matters. Your selfless dedication to other people is an inspiration to all who witness it. You are one of my greatest blessings in this life.

I am thankful for God's unexplainable, indescribable Grace!

Acknowledgments

Special thanks to my good friend Ed Slott and the entire team at Ed Slott and Company, LLC (www.irahelp.com). Your passion and desire are contagious. You are always giving back to others. I can't begin to explain the blessing you have been to me during the course of my financial planning career. I wouldn't trade the training or knowledge you continually pass on to me for anything. You are simply THE BEST!

Thank you to Nate Murphree, Brooke Sellers-Watson, and the team at Aegis Financial in Denver, Colorado. Thank you for introducing me to *Safe Money Radio* back in 2009. What a life-changing experience it has been. You are business partners, friends, and family. I am grateful for all of you. We make a great TEAM!

Thank you to Hunter, Faith, Autumn, and Ethan. You are the best children a father could ever ask for. I appreciate everything you stand for and the way you care for those around you. I am so proud of you! You bless my life tremendously.

Thank you to Michael DeLon and his team. You are truly wonderful people, and it is a blessing to work with you.

Finally, to August James Tyler Newman, Paw-Paw loves you more than anything in the world! I will always save the best seat for you—right next to me!

Foreword

Brad Pistole got a second chance at life. In the pages that follow, you will soon know why and see how he is using this extended life opportunity to share his life-saving prescription for protecting your retirement savings from tax and investment risk so you can keep and enjoy more of your hard-earned retirement savings.

I am both proud and honored to write this foreword for Brad because he has been on a sincere mission to help people create a safe and secure retirement. Lots of financial advisors say they do this, but they just don't. That's the reality. When it comes to your retirement savings, it's not about how much you have accumulated but what you get to keep *after* taxes. Unfortunately, the average financial advisor does not have the specialized skills and knowledge to do this kind of planning for you. I know this for a fact because over the past thirty years, my team of IRA experts and I have trained more financial and tax advisors in this highly specialized area than anyone in the country. I only wish we could reach more advisors like Brad, who value education and make it a priority in their planning business. This is why almost twenty years ago, I created Ed Slott's Elite IRA Advisor Group℠, which Brad references several times in this book. It's the highest level of IRA distribution training available, an ongoing education program for financial and tax advisors to address tax planning for retirement accounts, such as IRAs, 401(k)s, and other retirement plans.

Brad has been training and studying with us for over ten years and has reached our highest level by achieving membership in our Master Elite IRA Advisor Group. Now that is what I call a true lifetime commitment to education, and that's why his clients—and now you, his readers—are lucky. You get to capitalize on Brad's investment in his education. He can proudly call himself a specialist in helping you achieve your retirement dreams because he has (and still does) put in the time it takes to create tax planning solutions. His solutions will leave you with more money—not only to enjoy in retirement but more tax-free and guaranteed—which means more of it that can be passed on to your loved ones. He shows you how to remove Uncle Sam as your primary IRA beneficiary. You don't really want a joint account with Uncle Sam, do you?

This book is also valuable to you in another sense—timing. Brad takes you through the challenges of the 2020 (and 2021) COVID-19 pandemic and gives you rock-solid planning ideas to remove risk from your retirement savings in a post-COVID-19 world.

Because of the uncertainties that linger after the pandemic, people want to create more stable retirement plans that can withstand the next black swan event. What retirees need going forward is less risk and more guaranteed income in retirement. As I am writing this (April 2021), the market is riding high, reaching new heights almost every week. But that cannot go on forever, and at some point, the bubble will burst.

In addition, our national debt and deficit levels are skyrocketing off the charts, and Congress is considering big tax hikes that will likely impact your spending ability in retirement. In light of these events, the timely planning advice that Brad shares in these pages should be heeded and acted on sooner rather than later. In these unprecedented times of uncertainty, you need to position your life savings so you can sleep at night.

You've worked, sacrificed, and saved, and now you deserve to be able to reap the rewards of your years of effort.

The ideas in this book will help you do that by providing a volatility and tax buffer for your savings, sort of like a giant shock absorber to shelter your retirement funds from minor bumps to major craters. Or, as Brad says, your retirement savings need to be made "bulletproof" no matter what comes your way.

You should never have to worry about these uncertainties, and what you'll learn here is that you'll no longer have to. You have Brad! You have a specialist.

Ed Slott, CPA and retirement expert
Author and founder of www.irahelp.com
Founder of Ed Slott's Elite IRA Advisor Group^{SM}
April 27, 2021

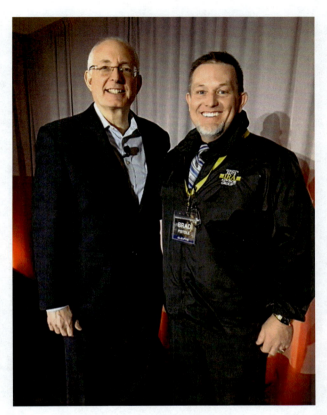

Keynote Speaker Ed Slott being introduced by Brad Pistole at the Aegis Financial National Advisors Summit in Denver, CO, on March 5, 2020.

Introduction

I opened my eyes on April 1, 1999, and Janet Jackson was standing over me. Although my mind struggled to process the surroundings, I recognized Janet. She was a nurse and the mother of two teens in my youth group. Janet wore scrubs and spoke directly to me. "Brad, Dr. Word wants to talk to you."

I also recognized Dr. Word. He was the father of two teenagers from the same youth group. Dr. Word appeared next to my bed, and with tears in his eyes, he placed his hand on my arm. I had never seen him cry before. "Brad, I have some really bad news," he said. "The scan we performed this morning revealed a brain tumor. I want you to speak to Dr. Queeny."

Surely this was a bad dream, right?

Unfortunately, this was not a dream. I was aware of Dr. Queeny also. He was the neurosurgeon who performed my grandfather's aneurysm surgery just one year ago. The young, confident surgeon entered my room. He confirmed what Dr. Word told me. A large, lemon-sized tumor was found on the left side of my brain. With authority, Dr. Queeny explained that although he would love to perform my surgery, he knew of a specialist who was explicitly trained to treat cases like mine and recommended that I see him. The specialist was only two and a half hours away at the University of Arkansas Medical Sciences Hospital in Little Rock.

Just ten days later, on a Monday morning, I found myself in the office of Dr. Al-Mefty. Sitting in the office lobby, I was surrounded by patients with brain tumor diagnoses. The nurse called me back and began asking what seemed like endless questions. I responded to her inquiries and paused.

"Just how serious is this?" I asked.

The nurse responded with, "You will know how serious this is based on how quickly Dr. Al-Mefty schedules you for surgery. His current surgical waiting list is over two months."

Dr. Al-Mefty entered the room and performed a rigorous examination. He checked my vision and physical response to stimuli and asked how long I had suffered from blurred vision and headaches. He was taken aback by my response. I had not experienced blurred vision, headaches, or dizziness. Dr. Al-Mefty explained that he had never seen a tumor the size of mine in a man my age; I was just twenty-seven years old and stunned at this revelation. As he continued, the doctor described the surgical procedure. He told me that small tumors are usually removed through the nasal cavity. However, my tumor was too large for that method. I would require an invasive procedure via entry into my skull.

My father, who was with me at the consultation, asked Dr. Al-Mefty one question. "If Brad was your son, what would you do?"

Dr. Al-Mefty quickly responded. "If Brad were my son, I would want to know that I did everything I could to remove the tumor." He then said, "I would like to schedule your surgery for this coming Thursday." I immediately remembered what the nurse had told me moments before about the seriousness of my condition. I had surgery just three days later.

On Thursday morning, April 15, 1999, I was in surgery by 11:00 a.m. That is one tax deadline day I will never forget! Nearly eleven hours later, the surgeons and doctors had successfully removed the benign meningioma tumor from my brain. My hospital recovery was expected to take up to two weeks, followed by several additional months of recovery at home. Yet, miraculously, I walked out of the hospital Sunday, just two and a half days later. Eleven days later, I returned to work.

We are all familiar with doctors. We begin our infancy with regular visits to our pediatrician. As we grow, we continue seeing a family practice physician or primary care doctor for our basic health care needs. It isn't until something significant happens, such as a tumor, a heart attack, or a cancer diagnosis, that we seek a specialist's services. When we need a knee or hip replaced, we find the best orthopedic surgeon in our area.

When you have a retirement account with tax-deferred funds in it, you have a special problem. Much like my brain tumor, you have a tax tumor that a primary care or general financial advisor is not equipped to handle. Financial planners are easy to find in every American town. They all claim to provide the same basic services and can give you access to investments, such as stocks, bonds, mutual funds, annuities, and life insurance. They are trained on various methods to get your money *INTO* an investment, but they have no idea how to get the money *OUT* of the investment in the most tax-efficient manner.

Very few financial advisors are trained IRA (Individual Retirement Arrangement) specialists, specifically trained to deal with the tax tumors inside your tax-deferred accounts. As a matter of fact, most advisors would claim that isn't even their job. Their job as your "investment specialist" is to make you money. They hang their hat on how big your return is each year. Most tell you to take any tax-related questions to your CPA. I couldn't disagree more. I have trained under Ed Slott, *America's IRA Expert* and the best CPA in the United States, for many years. I am an Ed Slott Master Elite IRA Advisor. I am a specialist. And I am here to help you remove the risk and the tax tumors that live inside your retirement accounts. I am here to help you eliminate the number one fear of every retiree: running out of money before running out of life. I will show you how to develop a *bulletproof* retirement income plan that is *safe* and *secure*, and it will provide an income stream that will last the rest of your life.

Brain scan showing tumor

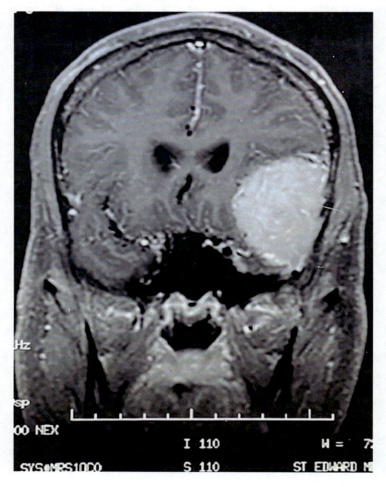

Post-surgery photos

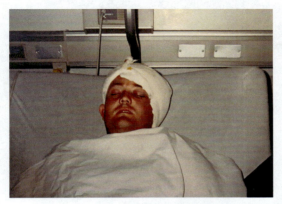

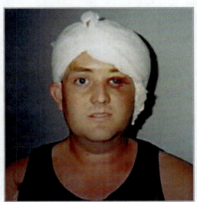

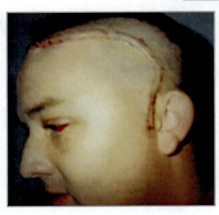

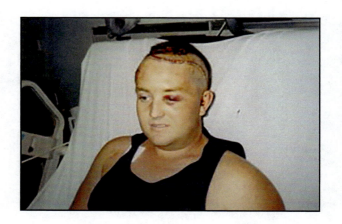

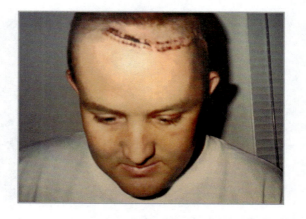

Chapter 1

Houston, We Have a Problem

> "We cannot solve our problems
> with the same thinking we used
> when we created them."
>
> —Albert Einstein

Since 2010, I have been the host of *Safe Money Radio*, which airs five times a week on several different stations in Missouri, Arkansas, and Kansas. If you've ever had the opportunity to listen to one of my shows, you will regularly hear me say one thing: When it comes to your retirement accounts and trying to "time the markets," good luck—because no one knows when the market will go up, and no one knows when the market will go down. Your broker doesn't know. Jim Cramer doesn't know. Dave Ramsey doesn't know.

Suze Orman doesn't know. I certainly don't know. No one knows! Do you know what the stock market crashes of 2001, 2008, and 2020 have in common? *No one saw them coming.* Things were rocking and rolling. The economy was doing great! Unemployment was at all-time record lows. The country's morale was strong! And then, virtually overnight: the stock market *crashed*! And when it did, it left millions of people financially and emotionally devastated. Especially those who had just retired and were relying on those accounts for their lifetime income.

In February of 2020, a major worldwide crisis appeared out of nowhere and took everyone by surprise. It was a new type of coronavirus named COVID-19. News of this unknown-illness-turned-worldwide-pandemic spread immediately, like a wildfire in California; the adverse effects of this news were immediate. In just twenty-three days of trading (from February 20–March 20, 2020), the Dow Jones dropped more than 11,000 points and was down more than 36 percent from the all-time high set in early 2020. If you were invested in the stock market or any other variable account that did not protect your principal, you probably lost more than 30 percent of your account values, so you know just how painful and frightening it was—especially if you were already retired or planning to retire soon.

During the first week of March 2020, before most airline travel in the United States came to a virtual halt, I was in Denver, Colorado, for a very special national conference for two hundred of the top US financial advisors. While I was there, I was blessed to spend two days with *America's IRA Expert*, Ed Slott. I had several one-on-one conversations with him. I also hosted a forty-five-minute interview with him that aired on *Safe Money Radio* and can be viewed on my website home page at GuaranteedSafeMoney.com. During the interview, we talked in depth about the SECURE Act—which President Donald Trump signed into law in December of 2019—and about COVID-19 and its impact on the markets and our worldwide economy at that time.

Ed was one of the keynote speakers at the conference. Right before we walked up on stage for me to introduce him, he was on his cell phone being interviewed by a major television network. The network called Ed because the markets were crashing: They wanted his opinion regarding the current state of the economy and how it was being affected by the novel coronavirus outbreak. During his talk to the financial advisors in Denver, he mentioned the extreme *volatility* of the markets. The day he spoke, the Dow dropped 970 points. But that was just a drop in the bucket compared to what it did during twenty-three consecutive days of trading from February 20 – March 20, 2020.

Just listen to these numbers from the stock market crash of 2020. Starting on February 20, 2020, the Dow dropped seven days in a row, losing 3,582 points. During the week of March 9 – March 13, the Dow lost 2,683 points. And between March 16 – March 20, the Dow dropped 4,011 points—the worst week on Wall Street since the 2008 financial disaster. The volatility during this month of trading was unlike anything that has ever existed. From February 20 – March 20, 2020, in just twenty-three days of trading, the Dow Jones lost over 11,000 points. It dropped from a fifty-two-week high of 29,568 in early 2020, to a low of 18,591 in late March. In fact, January 1 – March 31, 2020, was the worst first-quarter performance for the Dow Jones and the S&P 500 in the history of the stock market, leaving many shell-shocked investors!

Getting Caught with Your Retirement Pants Down

Here's an example of what an unexpected market crash can do to a retirement plan. In June of 2020,

I received a call from a longtime *Safe Money Radio* listener. She said the recent drop in the markets had crushed her retirement account, and she was extremely upset. She requested a free consultation and asked me to look at her most recent statement.

Her January 1 – March 31, 2020, quarterly statement told the story. On January 1, 2020, she had a value of **$410,012.61** in her 403(b). During the first quarter, she made contributions of **$6,164.20**, making the total **$416,176.81**. However, her investment loss during the quarter was $96,244.11, giving her a March 31, 2020, account balance of $319,932.70, which represented more than a 23 percent loss. She was down 14.06 percent for the last twelve months. But this wasn't the worst part of the news: This client wasn't a forty-year-old with plenty of time to allow the markets to recover. She was sixty-three and had already scheduled her retirement for January of 2021, only six months away. This kind of life event can leave you mentally and emotionally devastated. She wanted my help to get her retirement plan protected and moved back in the right direction (more on this in Chapter 6).

When it comes to retirement planning, one of the most difficult challenges retirees face is coming up with an income plan that will last the rest of their lives no matter how long they live. People simply cannot afford to base this plan on an advisor's opinion or the history of the past performance of some index or investment. Why? Because past performance and history mean absolutely nothing when facing the reality of a worldwide pandemic or an economic crash. When it comes to the income you will need to live on for the rest of your life, it needs to be based on *guarantees*. Life can change in the blink of an eye—and those changes can be devastating. Just ask anyone who was invested in the stock market or any other variable account in 2001, 2008, and 2020, and relied on those accounts to provide their retirement income.

People who enter retirement in today's world face several different risk factors, ones that can turn retirement plans upside down—and quickly. Years ago, I taught three-week retirement planning courses on various college campuses in Springfield and Ozark, Missouri, held at Drury University and Ozarks Technical Community College. One of the courses was titled "Financial Longevity for Retirement." During this course, we talked about the risks that retirees face today, including inflation and taxation eroding retirement savings; market downturns depleting the assets necessary for retirement income; the possibility of outliving assets and income; long-term care; and the risk of excessive taxation during the distribution of your estate. In other words, you simply must have a plan for *inflation, market volatility, longevity, health risks,* and *taxes.*

Best-selling author, economist, and public speaker Tom Hegna has shared some very valuable information with retirees on the importance of not getting caught with their retirement pants down, especially when in or near retirement.

Tom says:

> *One of the most interesting observations I've made during my study on retirement is that most of the public discourse about retirement is primarily focused on asset accumulation or building up retirement savings. Everyone is focused on their "pile of money." How big can I get the pile? But there has been very little discussion about retirement income.*
>
> *Retirees don't live on assets, they live on income! Your assets can be lost, they can be stolen, swindled, sued, divorced, or decimated in a market crash. The ultimate success of your retirement is not about assets. It's about income and risk management. This is a huge paradigm shift. It goes against EVERYTHING you have been doing up to this point.*

> *Let's pretend that you and your partner are now retired. You know what you need? You need a paycheck. You can have that paycheck guaranteed or not guaranteed. Which would you prefer?*
>
> *Now if you said guaranteed, how long do you want it guaranteed for—the rest of your life? Or for the rest of both your lives?*
>
> *If you answered guaranteed for the rest of both your lives, you need guaranteed lifetime income.*[1]

The problem with staring at your different piles of money is that no one knows what level of *income* they will provide in retirement. And what happens if you use your advisor's suggested 4 percent withdrawal rule in retirement (which is based on hypothetical returns and not guarantees), and then the markets experience more than a 30 percent drop as they did in 2001, 2008, and 2020? Are you willing to adjust your income and lifestyle while you wait on the markets and your retirement account to recover? What happens if they don't recover?

Tom Hegna says, "Losing money right before or right after retirement can devastate your entire

---

1 Tom Hegna, *Don't Worry, Retire Happy!* (Arizona: Tross Press, 2015), Preface x–xi.

retirement. This is why it is so important to have some guarantees in your portfolio."[2]

I couldn't possibly begin to count how many times I have received a call from a radio listener or potential client who called into the show to discuss the devastating losses in their retirement accounts. The conversation normally goes something like this: "Brad, I listened to your show, and I had no idea there were accounts that would protect my principal against losses. I've had my money with XYZ advisor for the past twenty years, and I lost a lot of money in 2001 and 2008. I simply can't afford to experience those losses again. I am too close to retirement, and I do not have the time to wait for my accounts to come back from a 30–40 percent loss. I am afraid of the current volatility of the markets, and I want to keep my money SAFE. I need this money to live on during my retirement years."

Do you have a similar story? Have you experienced major losses in your retirement accounts in 2001, 2008, and 2020? Are you retired or close to retirement and afraid the next market crash will keep you from living the retirement of your dreams? Keep reading.

---

2 Hegna, *Don't Worry, Retire Happy!* Preface xv.

Chapter 1: Summary and Questions

- Losing money from your retirement accounts when you are nearing retirement or already retired will destroy your retirement plan. This is especially true if you plan to start taking distributions from your account immediately.

- The amount of money in your retirement accounts is not what is important. What matters most is the amount of guaranteed lifetime income you have secured for your retirement.

- Hypothetical returns and hypothetical income projections will not give you the retirement of your dreams. Guaranteed income for life will let you sleep peacefully at night.

- Where was your money invested during the stock market crashes of 2001, 2008, 2020?

- Did you get caught with your retirement "pants down"?

- How does it make you feel when you watch your hard-earned money disappear from your accounts?

- Do you have retirement accounts that will guarantee you and your spouse lifetime income no matter how long you live? If not, WHY not?

Chapter 2

Pressing Your Luck

"Luck is merely an illusion, trusted by the ignorant and chased by the foolish."

—*Timothy Zahn*

The beginning of 2020 was unlike anything most of us have ever witnessed. I'm sure you can remember a time in your life when the train seemed to jump off the tracks, but 2020 seemed to take the cake. Who could have possibly foreseen a worldwide pandemic as a possibility for the new year? Flights were cancelled, sporting events were cancelled, business trips and vacations were cancelled; you name it, it was cancelled or postponed. Schools never reopened after spring break. Colleges shut down. Restaurants, businesses, libraries, and movie theaters closed. Churches and places of worship closed. Heck, even the IRS offices closed their doors. And don't even get me started on the masks and "social distancing." It was unlike anything any of us ever witnessed.

During this extended time at home, many people watched more television and movies than ever before. As a result, Netflix stock went through the roof. And in the midst of all of this COVID-19 *craziness*, the age-old game show *Press Your Luck* made its return to television. If you've ever watched *Press Your Luck*, you know all about playing games of chance with your money (and you know all about the WHAMMIES!). You can probably see those little red devil characters in your mind right now, along with the WHAMMY music that plays every time they come to take away all your money.

If you have not watched *Press Your Luck*, I highly recommend it. Because, whether you realize it or not, those of you who own 401(k)s (or any other type of retirement account held in a brokerage account) play this game every single day of your life.

When a contestant steps up to play *Press Your Luck*, they are looking at a large, constantly moving board, and they get to decide when to hit the STOP button. Once the board starts moving and the music starts playing, the excitement begins. And if you've ever watched the show, you know the little WHAMMIES pop up all over the board, changing locations very quickly, as the contestant shouts, "No WHAMMIES, no WHAMMIES, no WHAMMIES! Come on, big money! No WHAMMIES . . . STOP!" And when they hit stop, whatever they land on is what they get. It could be a prize, a specific amount of money, a free spin, or (you guessed it) a WHAMMY! If they land on a monetary amount or a prize, they can choose to keep going until they are out of spins, hoping to increase their winnings. If they choose to keep on playing, they say, "I'm going to *press my luck*." But, of course, if they decide to press their luck and land on a WHAMMY, they lose every single penny and every prize that's in their bank, and it starts back over at zero!

    I was watching the show one night and witnessed something incredible. A contestant *pressed his luck* throughout most of the show, and throughout several rounds, he built up over $125,000 in his account. The amazing thing was, he avoided the dreaded WHAMMY twenty-eight spins in a row! Wow! That was unheard of. Of course, he could have walked away with over $125,000 in cash and prizes, but instead, the adrenaline and greed took over, and he decided to *press his luck*. Guess what happened on the twenty-ninth spin? You guessed it! He went from over $125,000 to ZERO . . . *just like that*! He had two spins left, so, of course, he decided to PRESS HIS LUCK again. After all, he had made it twenty-eight spins in a row without a WHAMMY, and he had nothing to show for it. So, he decided to press on. He won money on the next spin, and then, the dreaded WHAMMY made yet another appearance, and he lost it all again. He went twenty-eight attempts without a WHAMMY—and then he lost it all in two of three attempts to "hit the jackpot."

Isn't that a lot like having your retirement money invested in the stock market? When it's going up, up, up, and there aren't any downturns, it has the tendency to *hook* you. It's like a magic rush of adrenaline! But then, all of a sudden, out of nowhere, the dreaded WHAMMY makes an appearance, and just like that, a huge portion of everything you have worked so hard for is suddenly GONE!

The Triple WHAMMY

Having a 401(k) invested in the market is like playing a real-life game of *Press Your Luck*. How many of you have handed your money over to an advisor and have been "letting it ride" on the up-and-down roller coaster that is the stock market?

You are busy working and raising a family, and you don't have the time or the training to watch your accounts every day.

If you are nearing your retirement date or are already retired, you are probably beginning to realize you need to start paying more attention to what's going on—especially when markets take massive drops as they did in 2001, 2008, and 2020. If you hit "stop" on your working career to begin the retirement of your dreams, and the market starts an unexpected crash, it is just like landing on a great big WHAMMY. You will risk losing a huge portion of what you have worked so hard to save and what you need for retirement income.

One of my mentors, Ed Slott, poses a great question: "Do you know what the difference is between lettuce and garbage? . . . TIMING!" Think about that for a minute. Your current retirement plan might look pretty good—especially if the markets are *up*. But what happens if your retirement plan was set for you to begin taking distributions in 2001, 2008, or the spring of 2020? And then, out of nowhere, your current investments land on a great big WHAMMY! Timing is everything. In fact, it is one of the only things that separates lettuce from garbage!

Take a closer look at the triple WHAMMY (and why avoiding it is so important if you want to have a *safe and secure retirement income plan*). I have been saying for years, "It's not what you MAKE; it's what you KEEP that counts." I learned this many years ago from Ed Slott.

Here is a great question: If you have $500,000 in your retirement account, and I have $500,000 in mine, who has more money? Does this sound like a trick question? Let me rephrase. If you have $500,000 in your IRA and I have $500,000 in my Roth IRA, who has more money? The correct answer: I do. A lot more money. How can this be? We both have a balance of $500,000 in our retirement account. Don't forget: "It's not what you make; it's what you keep that counts." If we both have $500,000 in our retirement accounts and we both retire and start taking income from the accounts at the same time, that's where the triple WHAMMY starts to rear its ugly head.

Let me show you how this works:

Let's suppose you and your advisor determine you'll need an annual distribution of $25,000 from your $500,000 account to combine with your Social Security payment and provide the income you need for retirement. This amount represents a 5 percent annual withdrawal from the $500,000 account. Once you start the withdrawal, this represents part one of the triple WHAMMY: *distributions*. As expected, distributions will affect your retirement accounts. Once you start taking a 5 percent distribution, you will need to make this percentage back in your investments to avoid running out of money before you run out of life.

Part two of the triple WHAMMY is *losses*. What happened to the people who retired in 2001, 2008, or more recently, in January 2020? If you retired in January of 2020 and started taking a distribution from your retirement account, you not only experienced the negative impact of the distribution, but you would have also experienced the negative impact of the losses to your account. If you had invested in an account that did not protect your principal, you might have lost as much as 35 percent because of market fluctuations. Add this 35 percent loss to the 5 percent distribution you took, and your account is now down 40 percent.

And let's not forget part three of the triple WHAMMY: *fees*. All brokerage accounts have fees charged against them to pay advisor and management fees. On average, the fee is 1 percent of the value of the account. However, I have seen them as high as 3 percent. Let's do some quick math. If you have a $500,000 account and start a $25,000 distribution (while concurrently experiencing a 35 percent loss and paying a 1 percent management fee), how much money will you have left at the end of the first year? You will not like the answer, but this is critical when planning for a *safe* and *secure* retirement income plan. The answer: $295,000. Wait! What? That can't possibly be right.

You might be thinking: *I only took out $25,000 from a $500,000 account; how could it possibly be down to $295,000 after just one year?* Answer: math. If you take a $25,000 distribution while experiencing a 35 percent loss and paying a 1 percent management fee on the $500,000 account, the triple WHAMMY will result in a $205,000 deduction from your account, leaving you with $295,000. Does this sound like a good plan to you?

Now you know why so many people who retired in 2001 and 2008 found themselves back at work a short time later. The triple WHAMMY will eat your lunch and leave you devastated—and must be avoided at all costs once you reach retirement.

This does not take into consideration one of the most overlooked parts of retirement planning: taxes. That's why Ed Slott continually says, "It's not what you MAKE; it's what you KEEP that counts." Let's not forget the original question I asked earlier: If you have $500,000 in your IRA and I have $500,000 in my Roth IRA, who has more money?

Assume your $500,000 IRA is invested in a brokerage account that does not protect your principal from losses. Then assume there is a 1 percent ongoing management fee charged against it. On the other hand, let's also assume that my $500,000 Roth IRA is invested in something that protects 100 percent of the principal and has NO annual management fee. Now, repeat the same distribution scenario and see which plan you would prefer for your retirement.

Assuming you retired in January of 2020 and started distributions from your $500,000 IRA, you would have experienced *distributions* ($25,000), *losses* (35 percent = $175,000), fees (1 percent = $5,000), and ... the TAXES that will be due on the $25,000 distribution from the tax-deferred IRA. This brings up a very important tax issue that most people don't realize until they retire and start their distributions from Social Security and their tax-deferred retirement plans. They realize their problem when they get their first tax bill from Uncle Sam. Since your $25,000 annual distribution from your IRA is a taxable distribution, it will also affect the income threshold associated with your Social Security distributions. In short, because of the taxable distribution from your IRA account, your Social Security income will also be taxed. Do not forget about taxes as you do your retirement income planning. Uncle Sam certainly won't! (https://www.irs.gov/newsroom/dont-forget-social-security-benefits-may-be-taxable)

Consider the following safe and secure retirement income plan. Assuming I retired in January of 2020 and started distributions from my $500,000 Roth IRA (which was protected from losses and fees), my $25,000 distribution would be the ONLY deduction from the account. Remember, I took the time to set up a BULLETPROOF plan. It is safe and secure, and it provides lifetime income for my family and me. And since I took the distribution from a Roth IRA, I wouldn't owe any federal or state taxes on the distribution. Therefore, the account balance after one year—even in a year in which the stock market dropped 35 percent—would still be **$475,000**.

> Question: Which retirement account would you prefer? The one with a balance of $295,000 (with taxes due on the $25,000 distribution) OR the account with a balance of $475,000 (with **no taxes due** on the $25,000 distribution)?

Remember, one of the only differences between lettuce and garbage is *TIMING*! Don't wake up and find your retirement plan in the garbage! You need a bulletproof plan that protects you from the dreaded triple WHAMMY and taxes. It needs to be safe and secure. And it needs to provide lifetime income for the rest of your life no matter what happens in the markets!

Chapter 2: Summary and Questions

- We now live in a post-pandemic world where taking risks might cost you more than ever before.

- Pressing your luck isn't a good financial planning strategy if you are near or in your retirement.

- Have you ever stopped long enough to realize that having a 401(k) invested in the markets is like playing a real-life game of *Press Your Luck*?

- Can you remember a time when you continued to press your luck in the stock market and landed on a great big WHAMMY? How did it make you feel?

- Have you ever experienced the triple WHAMMY = distributions + losses + fees?

- How did it feel to pay fees while your retirement account was losing money?

- It's not what you MAKE; it's what you KEEP that counts.

- Would you like a retirement plan that is SAFE and SECURE that guarantees you a lifetime income you can never outlive?

Chapter 3

Taking Inventory

"I finally know what distinguishes man from the other beasts: financial worries."
—Jules Renard

It has been said by many successful people throughout the years that to get something you've never had, you have to be willing to do something you've never done. Typically, it means you will have to do something most people do not want to do, something requiring hard (not fun) work. Was there ever a time in your life when you realized or admitted you were out of shape? If so, do you remember what those first few workouts were like when you started the painful process of exercising the muscles that had been neglected for a long time? It is not fun. And do you know why every single workout plan has a disclaimer? It goes something like this: *Always consult your physician before starting any exercise program.* You need to take an inventory of your current health status to develop the best plan for you and your specific situation.

Your financial situation is no different. You will have to take an inventory of your current financial plan to see if it will meet your retirement goals and needs. It is best to make sure you are using the assistance of a qualified professional to help you get where you want to go.

Have you ever witnessed or participated in a business inventory? If not, it is quite an experience. The following story illustrates the importance of taking inventory.

In the fall of 2020, I was working on a tractor at my farm when an unexpected event took place. When I moved the levers that unhook the bucket on the front of my tractor, I noticed that a (seemingly) insignificant nut was missing from a bolt. I was trying to take the bucket off the tractor to install forks that would allow me to move pallets. I expected to find the missing nut somewhere close by on the ground, but it was nowhere to be found. The seemingly insignificant little part turned out to be a BIG, BIG deal. That little nut held the bolt that went through the shaft on the bucket. Without it, the bolt would not stay in place, and therefore, neither the bucket nor the forks could be used to lift anything. So, I did what any good weekend farmer would do. I went to the shop and looked through every container of nuts and bolts I could find, hoping to find a replacement for the seemingly insignificant nut, but I didn't have any luck.

After an hour, I gave up. I took the bolt, hopped in the truck, and headed to Home Depot. After more than thirty minutes and with the help of the specialist in the nuts and bolts area, we determined the store did not carry that nut. So, I took my bolt and headed to the tractor supply store. Surely, they would carry a seemingly insignificant nut for a bolt that is on almost every single tractor on the market. However, after more than forty-five minutes with their specialist, we determined they did not carry that specific nut either. Frustrated, I asked the specialist if there was anywhere else in town that might carry that particular nut. He suggested a machine shop and gave me directions.

When I arrived at the machine shop, I noticed several cars and trucks outside the shop. I thought, *Wow! They are really busy!* And then I walked up to the doors and read the dreaded sign: "Closed for 2020 Inventory."

You have got to be kidding me; I was so frustrated! I cupped my hands and peered through the window, and then, thankfully, a man walked up behind me. He was carrying several boxes of doughnuts for the workers and said, "Can I help you?" I explained what I had been through and what I was looking for, and he said, "We are closed for our annual inventory, but come on in. I will see what I can do."

The staff searched high and low for the nut that would fit my bolt. Finally, a floor manager came out from the back and explained the situation. He said, "The problem is, this is a metric nut with a *fine* thread. It is very rare, and we hardly ever keep them in stock, but I will keep looking." And to the glory of God, he finally found one tiny box that contained the nut to fit the bolt on my tractor. I was so thankful! It was like he found a gold nugget worth millions of dollars.

When he asked me how many I wanted, I said, "I'll take the whole box." I certainly did not want to experience what I had just been through ever again, so I wanted to make sure I had spares in my possession.

I was inside the machine shop for more than thirty minutes, and during that time, I talked to the owner and learned a lot about the importance of taking an annual inventory. I was blown away by all that is involved in taking an accurate inventory and just how important it is for running a successful business. It made me think a lot about financial planning and how important it is to begin your safe and secure financial plan with a very thorough financial inventory.

It is interesting how something that seems so insignificant can become important. When you are working and saving, *SAFETY* does not seem like it should be a priority. In fact, most investors never factor safety into their clients' retirement and investment plans. Most money managers are focused on *GROWTH*, and they promote their value by talking about how much money they can make you if they are your advisor. Their focus and value are based on the rate of return they can get you.

Depending on your age, this can be very important. However, when you reach a certain age in life, growth should become less important, and the safety of your accounts should become a major priority. For most retirees, the number one fear they face is running out of money before they run out of life. And when that is the case, the safety of your money should be your number one priority, followed closely by having accounts that will provide lifetime income to you and your spouse.

During every initial meeting I have with a potential client who has asked for a free consultation, I talk to them about the four purposes for money. When they ask to meet with me, they normally have a pot of money in mind they want to discuss. It might be a 401(k) they want to roll over to an IRA because they have left a job or are about to retire and don't want to leave their money with their former company. It might be a brokerage account that makes them nervous because it keeps fluctuating with the stock market. Or it might be money that is sitting in the bank making "gumball" money. You know what that is, right? If you give your money to a bank and let it sit for a year, you will make enough money to buy a package of gum—if you are lucky!

No matter the situation, people who have read my first book, *Safe Money Matters: Finding Safe Harbor in a Storm-Filled World*, or listened to my show, *Safe Money Radio*, for very long will normally walk into my office, hand me a copy of whatever account they want to discuss, and say something like, "Brad, I've been listening to your show for years, and I've read your book, so where should I put my money?"

And I will respond the same way every single time—by looking them straight in the eyes and saying, "I have no idea! I understand that you've been listening to my show for years, and you've read my book, but I just met you. The answer to that question depends on the answer to the question I am about to ask you. What is your primary purpose for this pot of money?"

There are only four main purposes for money. And you might like the sound of all four, but when it comes to moving a particular bucket of money, its purpose should dictate where you put it. I always advise my clients by saying, "Tell me the purpose for your bucket of money, and I will tell you where you should put it."

The four purposes for money include:

❶ **Safety**

❷ **Growth**

❸ **Income (for life)**

❹ **Estate Planning**

It is time to take an inventory of your accounts. First, think about each bucket of money you have and ask yourself why it is invested the way it is. Then ask yourself if that specific account or investment will meet the purpose you have for that money.

Most people have their money invested in a particular account because a broker or advisor told them to put it there. Often, retirees do not know what they are invested in. The most common thing I hear from the people I meet is: "I don't even know what I'm invested in. I have worked hard and have had the money automatically deducted from my paychecks. I feel bad to say this, but I have no idea what my money is invested in. I just know that when I look at my statements, the total goes up and down. And the fluctuation makes me nervous." I am certain many of you can relate to this.

If you truly want to develop a *safe and secure retirement income plan* that will work for you and your family for the rest of your lives, you will have to do some work. You must take an inventory and decide what you want to accomplish with your different buckets of money.

A great place to begin is by asking yourself, "What is my primary purpose for this money?" Is it safety? Is it growth? Do you need this money to provide lifetime income for you and a spouse? Perhaps this bucket of money is not needed for income, and you want to make sure it passes on to your family in the most tax-efficient way possible, which is *estate planning*.

Most of the time, I meet with couples who have multiple accounts. It might include 401(k)s and possible IRAs or Roth IRAs for each of them. I will often say, "It's OK if you have different purposes for different accounts. And one of you may have one primary purpose in mind, and your spouse might have a different one. My job is to help you determine the primary purpose for each account to make sure we are putting the money into accounts that meet those goals."

I have over one thousand clients, ranging in age from their mid-twenties to their mid-nineties. Most of my clients are in the fifty-five to seventy-five age range. Without exception, when I ask new clients what the purpose is for their money, more than 90 percent say, "My number one purpose for this money is safety, followed closely by income for life."

What is your purpose for your retirement money? Is it safety, growth, income, or estate planning? Do you have multiple buckets of money with more than one purpose for each one of them? Once you take an inventory of your accounts and know the answer to these questions, a qualified advisor will know exactly where to put that money.

You need to decide how you want to live and how long you want to work. If you fail to come up with the right financial plan and spend everything you make, you will have to work longer. On the other hand, if you invest in your future now by taking inventory and developing the right financial plan, you will have complete control over when you work and when you retire. Then you can travel more or do whatever you want, which represents true freedom. The choice is 100 percent up to you. Make the decision, commit to it, and live the life of your dreams.

Chapter 3: Summary and Questions

- Having the retirement of your dreams requires planning and dedication to the right plan.

- Before you can establish the appropriate plan for your retirement, you have to take a financial inventory of your retirement accounts.

- The four purposes for money are *safety, growth, income (for life), and estate planning.*

- Have you ever taken a financial inventory?

- Do you know why you are currently invested the way you are?

- What is the purpose for each bucket of money you have?

- Will your current investments allow you to reach those goals?

- Are your current investments insured or guaranteed? Why or why not?

- Are you willing to do whatever it takes to develop a safe and secure retirement income plan for you and your family?

Chapter 4

Laying the Right Foundation

**"Vision without execution
is just hallucination."**

—*Henry Ford*

You probably remember stories from your childhood that taught you how important it is to lay the right type of foundation before you build anything, especially a home. In fact, you might even remember a song about it that you probably learned in Sunday school. Do you know this one?

The wise man built his house upon the rock.

The wise man built his house upon the rock.

The wise man built his house upon the rock, and the rains came tumbling down.

Oh, the rains came down as the floods came up.

The rains came down as the floods came up.

The rains came down as the floods came up, and the wise man's house stood FIRM.

If you know that song, I am sure you are singing it in your head right now. And if so, you know what is coming in the second verse.

The foolish man built his house upon the sand.

The foolish man built his house upon the sand.

The foolish man built his house upon the sand, and the rains came tumbling down.

Oh, the rains came down as the floods came up.

The rains came down as the floods came up.

*The rains came down as the floods came up, and the foolish man's hou*se went SPLASH!

That simple and yet fun little song taught us the importance of laying the right type of foundation *before* starting to build anything. (Those truly were the "good ole days." I miss them.)

One of the most important things that will help you develop a *Bulletproof, Safe and Secure Retirement Income Plan* is knowing what kind of retirement planning ammunition is available to you. If we learned anything in late 2020 and early 2021, it was that just because you have a weapon, it does not mean you are prepared for battle. You also need AMMUNITION for that weapon.

If you are a gun owner, you found out just how hard it was to purchase ammo in a post-Trump political world. And it did not matter what kind of gun it was. Virtually overnight, ammunition sales went through the roof, and production stopped! It did not matter what store you walked into; you would have learned very quickly that there was a "new norm" regarding gun and ammunition sales. What was this "new norm"? Guns and ammunition became virtually nonexistent. Don't believe me? Just walk into a Walmart or an Academy Sports and go to the gun department. Look at the shelves where the guns *used* to be kept. In early 2021, those shelves were EMPTY! Then walk to the part of those stores that used to display the bullets and ammunition for dozens and dozens of weapons; those shelves now contain camping equipment. The days of walking into a store and buying ammo are gone.

What is more important: the gun or the ammo? I learned a very valuable lesson many years ago. The very first pistol I ever purchased was a .357 Magnum revolver. The ammo I bought would often get stuck in the revolver, and it would jam. Then I learned a very valuable piece of information from a specialist. He owned a gun store and knew things that most people never even learn. He asked me if I had ever used .38 Special ammo in my .357 revolver. I thought to myself: *What a foolish question. I already told him my gun is a .357 revolver. Why is he asking me if I have ever used .38 special ammo in my .357?*

So, I said, "No, I haven't."

He said, "You can shoot .38 Special ammo through a .357, and a lot of people find they like it even better than .357 ammo."

I thought, *surely this can't be true. Why haven't I ever heard this before? In fact, I've never heard anyone say that you can shoot .38 special ammo through a .357.* So, I asked around. After all, I didn't want to attempt to shoot .38 special ammo through a .357 revolver just because someone said you could. What if they didn't know what they were talking about? I could blow my hand off. Then, after doing my research, I learned that you could, in fact, shoot .38 Special bullets through a .357 revolver. So, I tried it. And guess what? It worked perfectly! In fact, the .38 Special bullets performed so much better that I stopped buying .357 bullets and stocked up on .38 special ammunition. And when the "run on ammo" occurred in 2021, and it was virtually impossible to find ammo anywhere, I found .38 Special ammo (and I purchased a considerable amount of it). Now I have a weapon in my arsenal that will perform in a way most people don't know about. Just think about how many people own .357 revolvers and don't know you can shoot .38 special bullets through them, and those people can't find .357 ammo. They are stuck! How effective is a gun without bullets?

I realized many years ago that it is priceless when you know things that other people don't know. Knowledge isn't power. *Applied knowledge* is power! And this is especially true when it comes to developing a safe and secure retirement income plan for your family! Knowing what other people do not know (and knowing how and when to apply those principles) can be life changing. Consider these quotes:

> "Ignorance deprives people of freedom because they do not know what alternatives there are. It is impossible to choose to do what one has never heard of."
> —Ralph B. Perry

> "Beware of false knowledge; it is more dangerous than ignorance."
> —George Bernard Shaw

> "Ignorance is never out of style. It was in fashion yesterday, it is the rage today, and it will set the pace tomorrow."
> —Frank Dane

> "Nothing in the world is more dangerous than sincere ignorance and conscientious stupidity."
> —Martin Luther King, Jr.

One of the most famous sayings of all time is "*Ignorance is bliss.*" Nothing could be further from the truth. I assure you. It is NOT bliss! Ignorance is painful. Ignorance leads to a long list of things, such as poor health, poverty, addiction, bankruptcy, broken relationships, and a lifetime of heartaches.

Secret Ammunition for Your Retirement Income Plan

When it comes to retirement planning and tax-deferred accounts, such as 401(k)s, 403(b)s, and thrift savings plans (TSPs), the list of terms and rules for making contributions and taking withdrawals can seem endless and overwhelming. This is especially true when you have a full-time career, are raising a family, and simply do not have the time or energy to keep up with the constant changes taking place. That is why most people hire a professional who specializes in these rules and regulations to help keep them moving in the right direction and to prepare them for retirement when that day comes.

Think about this for a minute; there are currently more than 10,000 people turning sixty-five every single day in this country. That is more than 10,000 people who are entering the world of retirement and Medicare every day. That means a massive amount of people are facing an endless list of retirement planning questions they don't know the answers to, and this can be very stressful.

People often ask what the number one thing is radio show listeners ask me when they call in to my show. Most callers are trying to learn how to keep their money protected from violent market swings because they have reached an age where they can no longer afford to go through a major *bear market*. (A bear market refers to a prolonged period of price declines in indexes, such as the Dow Jones or S&P 500. This term is most often used when a sustained loss of twenty percent or more occurs over a given period of time, like it did in 2001 and 2008.) As a result, investors do not have the time to recover from losses and fees like they did when they were younger. This is especially true if they are already taking distributions from their accounts.

Remember, **Distributions + Losses + Fees = the formula for what I call the Triple WHAMMY!** And this does not even include the TAXES that will be due for taking those distributions. Avoid this deadly combination at all costs in retirement. Just ask anyone who retired in 2001 or 2008. They will tell you what the triple WHAMMY combined with TAXES will do to a retirement plan.

When retirees call me, they ask questions about all kinds of topics, such as:

- How to avoid 10 percent penalties on distributions
- Roth conversions
- Required minimum distributions
- Qualified charitable distributions
- Tax planning
- Estate planning
- How to make their money last for the rest of their lives

But of all the things I get asked, I can tell you this, the most often missed retirement planning strategy (because people are simply unaware that it is available) is the *age fifty-nine and a half in-service withdrawal.* I have been writing about it and talking about it for years, yet every week, I come across people who have never even heard of this strategy. Most employees who have an active *defined contribution plan*, such as a 401(k) or a 403(b), can take advantage of it once they turn fifty-nine and a half. It has to be specified in the company plan document, but it has been my experience that this is available to employees about 95 percent of the time.

What is an *in-service withdrawal*? It is a qualified distribution you can take from your company plan while still employed by that company, and if you move the money the right way, it is not a taxable distribution. It will allow you to do a direct transfer or rollover of up to 100 percent of your vested funds to the account and custodian of your choice. And yes, even though you still work for your company and have an active retirement plan, such as a 401(k) or 403(b), you can move any vested funds out of those accounts to a new account, one you and your advisor feel will best meet your current and future retirement planning needs.

This transfer/rollover does not close your current account, even if you move 100 percent of the funds inside it, making your current balance zero. Your company plan will remain open. You can continue your payroll deposits into that account with your next paycheck, and you will continue to receive any available company matching funds.

It can be a very powerful planning strategy for your future retirement. Why? Here are a few of the main reasons an *age fifty-nine and a half in-service withdrawal* might benefit you at this stage in your retirement planning:

1. Once you reach age fifty-nine and a half, *your risk level should be decreasing* (especially if you plan to retire in the next few years). The in-service withdrawal will allow you to move any amount of money—up to 100 percent—from your current company plan to an account that is custom fit for your specific situation. Any amount of money you move via the in-service withdrawal can be structured to protect you from market risk and market volatility. The funds that remain in the company plan and all future payroll deposits, including the company match, can still participate in the market. Having more than one account can help you create a good mixture of potential growth and safety, giving you a more balanced portfolio.

2. This qualified distribution/rollover is *not taxable when done correctly*. There is no mandatory 20 percent withholding or 10 percent penalty on the distribution (like there is prior to age fifty-nine and a half). The funds will be moved to a qualified, tax-deferred account, and there is no taxable income reported to the IRS.

3. Company plans often have limited investment options. A rollover *can offer you several things that are not available inside your company plan*, such as:

   a. An increased number of investment options offered by the new custodian

   b. Fixed income options that protect you from market fluctuation

   c. Guaranteed income options that come with certain types of annuities offered by various insurance companies

   d. The ability to move funds from a company plan to an IRA. Individual retirement accounts have benefits and features that company plans do not offer and vice versa. (Always ask a qualified advisor if an IRA would be a better fit for your specific situation.)

4. This strategy *can provide income now* if you need it. Distributions from a company plan have a mandatory 20 percent tax withholding. Rolling over funds to an IRA will avoid this 20 percent withholding. Any funds moved into an IRA can immediately be used for income (without a 10 percent penalty or forced tax withholding). You can decide to

withhold taxes from the distribution from the IRA or not.

5. *Future income planning.* Moving funds to an IRA can allow you to secure a guaranteed source of future income. When structured correctly, your new account can avoid 100 percent of the volatility that often comes with the investment options inside your company plan; you can secure a contractual, guaranteed rate of return, which can be used for single or joint lifetime income in the future. *This* will protect you and your spouse from ever having to worry about running out of money in retirement. The paycheck from your rollover account can be structured to last the rest of *both* of your lives, no matter how long you live.

6. *Required minimum distribution (RMD) planning.* Tax-deferred accounts have various rules on when your required minimum distributions begin. Having retirement money in both a company plan and an IRA can offer you multiple options for dealing with Uncle Sam and the tax-infested distributions he will require from you in the future.

When I talk to people planning for their future retirement, I will often mention a strategy or tax planning concept they have never heard of before—which is especially frustrating to them after working with a financial advisor for thirty-plus years. Clients will often say, "Sometimes you just don't know what you just don't know. I wish I would have heard about this many years ago."

Like many other things you learn about in life, the age fifty-nine and a half in-service withdrawal might be one of those things you wish you had heard about long before now. However, what matters most is that you take the time to study this option now that you are aware of it and put it into place in your financial plan if it is a good fit for you. It could give you several options that were not available to you before learning about this great retirement planning strategy. If you are not sure if your company offers in-service withdrawals, reach out to a qualified advisor and talk to your HR department. Hopefully, this will put a new arrow in your quiver and give you another weapon that will help you take aim at the best retirement possible for you and your family.

Who knows, maybe you are fifty-nine and a half or older and had no idea this was even available to you. Perhaps you thought you were "stuck" until you retired or left your current job. And now you have found the right foundation for beginning your own *safe and secure retirement income plan*. Maybe you just found a .38 Special bullet that will shoot through the .357 Magnum that you thought was useless to you. When you lay a *safe* and *secure* foundation for your retirement plan and build on top of it with tools and materials that others are not aware exist, you will quickly realize you are on the path to the retirement of your dreams. Remember, knowledge is not power. *Applied knowledge* is power. Make sure you have the right ammunition for your safe and secure retirement income plan. It will help you put as many strategies as possible to work for you, and you will watch your retirement options increase overnight.

Chapter 4: Summary and Questions

- The foundation is the most important part of anything you choose to build.

- The wise man built his house upon the rock. The wise man's house stood FIRM.

- The foolish man built his house upon the sand. The foolish man's house went SPLASH!

- Ignorance isn't bliss; it leads to a lifetime of heartache.

- Have you ever heard of an age fifty-nine and a half in-service withdrawal?

- Did you know you can transfer tax-deferred accounts, such as 401(k)s, 403(b)s, and TSPs into a safe and secure retirement income account, and it is not a taxable event?

- Did you know you can take advantage of this strategy even if you are still working for your current employer if you have reached age fifty-nine and a half and they allow in-service withdrawals?

- Have you felt nervous or anxious about the level of risk and fluctuation in your 401(k) because you are too close to retirement to go through another bear market?

- Did you know other options are available to you that will allow you to eliminate these risks now and give you a custom-fit retirement plan?

Chapter 5

Choosing the Right Retirement Vehicle for Your Family

"The quickest way to double your money is to fold it over and put it in your back pocket."
—*Will Rogers*

In the spring of 2020, I found myself in a situation, one I did not want to be in. I owned a truck that I loved, but I had to face facts. My truck could no longer get me where I wanted and needed to go. I have been driving a four-wheel-drive truck since I was eighteen years old. And I will drive a truck until the day I die. But if I have learned anything in life, I can assure you of this one thing: Not all trucks are created equally. Just because you're in a truck, it doesn't mean you will end up at your intended destination. I can't tell you how many times I've been *stuck* in a truck, a long way away from any type of help. Once, I was stuck in the mud in a four-wheel-drive truck in a place without cell service when it was below freezing. And I was a long way away from any town. That was a fun day!

You know, a four-wheel drive comes in handy in lots of situations, but I have learned that these vehicles are (basically) helpless in *deep mud*. Thankfully, after several hours of trying to free it the normal way, I realized I had enough tools in my truck to disassemble part of an old barn. I used the wood from that barn to dig out small trenches in front of and behind my tires. Then, I used additional wood and some cinder blocks to fill the trenches, and I was finally able to get enough traction to get it out of the mud.

In the spring of 2020, when I realized my current truck could no longer get me where I needed to go, I made a decision I did not want to make. I had to get a new vehicle, one that is *built* to get me to where I need to go. I own two farms, and one of them has some steep terrain and deep draws. And my old truck would always scrape the front and back end every time I went through my valleys. I did this so many times it started to create some serious damage to the truck's frame, eventually breaking the brush guard on the front and bending the bumper and trailer hitch on the back.

I finally realized there was no way around it, and I purchased a new truck—but not just any truck. It was a very special truck, a *one-of-a-kind* type of truck, the kind that everyone stops and stares at. In fact, I think it's the most incredible truck I've ever seen. People walk all the way across parking lots at gas stations and stores just to look at it and ask me where I got it. And they roll their windows down at stoplights just to say, "Wow, I love your truck!"

But listen closely: That is not why I bought the truck. I bought it because I needed the *right vehicle* to get me to where I needed to go. This truck has a lift kit on it, so it sits up much higher than the previous truck. It also has a much bigger engine in it. So, I no longer deal with all the problems I had with my previous truck. I honestly don't know how I ever made it without the vehicle I have now. My new truck was designed to do the things I need to do, and it gets me everywhere I need to go.

Did you know the same things are true about retirement accounts? Some investments and retirement products look good on the outside, but they might not be designed to get you to where you want to go. And trust me, if you ever find yourself in the wrong retirement vehicle, it is more painful than being stuck in the mud! When you find yourself in the wrong retirement vehicle, you risk running out of money, not being able to afford the kind of life you expected to live, paying unnecessary taxes and unnecessary fees, and not being able to pass on an inheritance to your spouse and your children and grandchildren.

Once I was in the new truck, I recognized just how important it is to have the *right vehicle* to get you to where you want to go. And I realized just how much that relates to retirement planning. There are so many choices when it comes to investing your money for retirement (and lots of "retirement vehicles" to choose from). While some of these vehicles might be very popular and pushed by lots of advisors, they simply will <u>not</u> get you where you want to go in retirement. Before you decide what type of vehicle you want to use to accomplish your retirement goals, ask yourself, "*What is my purpose for this money?*" In other words, what are you trying to accomplish, and what is your final destination? I have been saying this for more than ten years on *Safe Money Radio*, and I say it to my clients during every income planning meeting: "*The purpose of money dictates its position.*" When you tell me your purpose for a particular bucket of money, I can tell you what type of account you should put it in.

For example, if the purpose of your retirement account is to provide monthly lifetime income for your family, you'll want to keep your money *safe* so that you can use it for that specific purpose. If you say, "I will probably never use this money. I want to pass it on to my heirs," that is a different purpose. If you say, "I am OK with *risk*, and I want to be aggressive with this account and grow it as much as I possibly can," that is a different purpose than the previous two. And those answers will dictate what type of vehicle you should use to accomplish your purpose. If you meet with someone about your retirement money and they don't ask you about your purpose for the money, you should run the other way. How could they possibly do what is in your best interest if they never ask you what your goals are for a particular account? It means they already knew what they were going to advise you to do (which is not what is in your best interest). Remember, not all financial vehicles are created equally. They all have different purposes, and some of them will not get you to your desired destination. You must be 100 percent sure you are picking the *right financial vehicle* for your retirement account, one that will take you where you need and want to go!

One Size Does Not Fit All

If you read my first book, *Safe Money Matters: Finding Safe Harbor in a Storm-Filled World*, you know I own five annuities and ten life insurance policies. Yes, that is not a typo. And I know what you might be thinking: *Annuities . . . yuck. Isn't that a four-letter word? I hear the "experts" like Suze Orman, Dave Ramsey, and all the big brokerage firms say to stay away from annuities. And life insurance? Are you serious? Isn't life insurance for the people who get to use your money once you pass away? Why would I want to put my retirement money into life insurance? I want to use my money for my own income.* Does any of this sound familiar?

One of the most difficult things is trying to teach someone how to do something they have done a certain way throughout their life in a different way. That is especially true if they do not even know why they believe something and simply do what they do "just because." You know what that means, right? It is just because someone else taught them to do it that way many years ago. This has never been truer than when it comes to financial planning. Most people spend their entire adult lives working forty-plus hours a week and raising a family. The last thing in the world they have the time or desire to do is stay up late at night trying to sift their way through the IRS tax code or attempting to formulate the best strategy for their future retirement plan. They normally trust the advice of the "expert" they hired to take care of those things for them. And they trust their advice is good and given with their best interest in mind. Sadly, this is often not the case.

Since 2008, I have written more than 1,000 annuities and life insurance policies for more than a thousand clients. I have clients in Missouri, Arkansas, Kansas, Oklahoma, Tennessee, Texas, Arizona, California, Iowa, and Florida. Keep in mind, any advisor with the appropriate licenses can write an annuity or life insurance contract for their clients—and they do not have to have any other special training or designations to do it. In fact, most of them do not. They simply have their license to do business and to represent certain products and accounts.

I am a Certified Financial Fiduciary® (CFF), a Certified Annuity Specialist® (CAS), and an Ed Slott Master Elite IRA Advisor group member. These special designations set me apart from others who simply have their licenses to present certain products. There is a big difference between the two types of advisors. Let me explain.

The CAS designation is issued by the Institute of Business & Finance (IBF) through a six-module program. The course includes three exams and a case study administered by the Financial Industry Regulatory Authority (FINRA). Candidates must complete the following requirements to obtain a CAS designation:

- Prerequisite: a bachelor's degree or two thousand hours of financial services work experience
- Complete a self-study program of six modules
- Pass three exams and a case study
- Complete continuing education requirements of thirty hours every two years

The IBF created the designation in 2006 to focus on building financial advisors' knowledge of annuities. Advisors who complete the course and receive the CAS designation will "develop a strong working knowledge of traditional fixed-rate, equity-indexed, and variable annuities, annuity contracts and titling options, living benefits, compound interest, and unnecessary taxes, and litigation issues" and "master sophisticated portfolio theory that top financial advisors use to evaluate new annuity products and riders."[3]

---

3 "Overview." Institute of Business & Finance. Accessed May 28, 2021. https://icfs.com/certified-annuity-specialist.

In addition to my CAS training and designation, I am also a Certified Financial Fiduciary®, "a professional designation for financial professionals, namely those who have successfully completed a rigorous certification and training process established by NACFF and AFEA (The American Financial Education Alliance), and who agree to uphold the highest moral, ethical and fiduciary standards of service when providing investment advice to potential and existing clients. . . . The NACFF has established strict criteria for becoming a Certified Financial Fiduciary® (CFF). CFF is not for everyone, and all fiduciaries are not the same. The CFF designation was established to identify the new standard of excellence amongst financial professionals who act as fiduciaries."[4]

Perhaps the most important of my training involves sitting at the feet of best-selling author and CPA Ed Slott. In his book, *Stay Rich for Life!*, Ed says, "There is one group of advisors that I know has made the commitment to continuing education in the distribution and taxation of retirement accounts. Why? Because they belong to Ed Slott's Elite IRA Advisor Group, an advanced learning program for select advisors who believe in investing in their own professional education so they

---

[4] National Association of Certified Financial Fiduciaries. Accessed May 28, 2021. https://nationalcffassociation.org/faq.

can do the best overall job for their clients. They are listed on my website at www.irahelp.com, and there are hundreds of them all over the country."

He then goes on to say, "Beware of the glossy brochures and of advisors, especially those at big brokerage firms and banks, who say they get their training and education 'in-house.' That kind of training and education is meaningless to you in terms of the big picture because it tends to focus on how to sell you products and services. That's fine, but it's not enough to help you create a well-thought-out financial plan."[5]

Even though many people offer their clients financial products and services, they are not all created equally. Far too often in my financial planning career, people who had already purchased an annuity or life insurance policy from someone else have called into my office after being referred or hearing me on the radio. The problem is that they never hear from the person who sold them that product again. Most of the time, this client will have attended a "free dinner seminar" or a "Social Security or retirement planning workshop" and then accepted the "free financial consultation" the advisor offered them. In just a matter of days after that meeting (and often after the very first meeting

---

5   Ed Slott, *Stay Rich for Life!:Growing & Protecting Your Money in Turbulent Times* (New York, Ballantine Books, 2009), 29.

with the advisor), the client will have moved a significant portion of their life savings into the product or investment the advisor suggested to them after their free consultation.

These clients then call me because they want a free review of what they had already purchased from another advisor. Most of the time, they have little to no idea of what they now own. Frequently, we find out that the "advisor" who moved their money is no longer in business or lives in another state. It is big business for financial groups to send out mass mailouts. (*Have you ever received a free dinner invitation in the mail?*) Then, at the appointed time, an advisor will show up in a city or state they do not even live in, host a free dinner event at a local restaurant a couple of nights in a row, and book as many "free consultations" as they can with attendees. In the following days, the advisor will meet—in homes or rented office space—with attendees who accepted their consultation offer and move as much of their retirement money as possible into the accounts that *they already planned on offering the dinner attendees before even meeting them.* Clients will not know until they get the first quarterly or annual statement that the advisor they gave their hard-earned money to lives in another state (or perhaps even halfway across the country), and they often learn the hard way that their advisor never had any intention of meeting with them again. Some advisors are in business to genuinely help their clients, and other advisors are in business for one reason: to do what they think is best for themselves—*making money*! Those advisors do not last long, and they leave retirees in a financial mess with no one to help them along the way. I wonder, just how much did that "free dinner" cost the attendee?

Here is another popular method that many salespeople disguised as "advisors" use to get into the pockets of retirees. When a retiree purchases a new home, their bank or mortgage lender will send countless letters to the home buyer, suggesting they buy a life insurance policy as "mortgage protection." (*How many times have you received this letter?*) I purchased a home in 2014 and paid it off within two years, and I *still* receive these solicitation letters in the mail, even though I have no mortgage balance. They have spent a small fortune trying to get me to meet with them.

If the homeowner accepts this offer and responds to the letter, the bank or mortgage company will send a "financial professional" to their home to meet with them. This person will talk to the homeowner about establishing the life insurance policy detailed in company correspondence. Then, before the meeting is over, the "financial professional" will find a creative way to ask the homeowner if they own any retirement accounts or CDs. Before the homeowner knows it, their bank or mortgage lender representative (who wanted to make sure you had coverage to pay off your mortgage in case of an emergency) magically turns into a "financial advisor" in the blink of an eye. And they will sell the homeowner an annuity or some other financial product before they can take their next breath.

Unfortunately, there is no financial or fiduciary integrity involved in this process; it has nothing to do with offering something in the homeowner's best interest. Keep in mind that this financial professional-turned-financial advisor doesn't know anything about the homeowner's retirement plans. I cannot tell you how many people who contact me asking for a free financial review are doing so because they have been sold a financial product by someone they met in their home after responding to a mortgage protection letter. Their stories are almost always the same: *"I'm not sure what I own, and I've never heard from the person who sold it to me since the day they were here."* If I took the time to share the heartbreaking stories of the many people I have met over the years who were sold a big pile of *junk* from the "advisor" or "financial professional" who came to their house, I would have to write another book dedicated to it alone.

When you meet with a Certified Financial Fiduciary®, you will immediately notice the difference. A CFF has taken an oath to *do what is ethical, moral, and in your best interest at all times.* They will always take the proper time to determine your primary purpose for moving retirement money into any account or investment. It might take three to four meetings; it might take three to four months. When you are searching for the best financial vehicle for you and your family, take your time. Finding the right vehicle also means finding the right financial professional to help you throughout the process. It should be very apparent if the person you are talking to is an advisor or a salesperson. There is a big difference. A fiduciary will do what is in your best interest; a salesperson will do what is in theirs. Personally, I follow the philosophy of my friend and mentor Ed Slott, a CPA and *America's IRA Expert,* who often says, "*Doing what is in your client's best interest is ALWAYS in your best interest.*"

When you step onto a car lot to find the right vehicle for you and your family, you might often be standing in a lot directly across the street from another car lot. In fact, they might even be selling the same vehicles. So how in the world would you know which car lot to pick? Isn't a Ford F-150 the same no matter what car lot you purchase it from? Maybe so. I suppose you probably choose the car lot for several reasons. Maybe they have been in business the longest and have the best reputation in that area. Maybe a friend of yours purchased a vehicle there and referred you to them because they trust them. Maybe you have purchased a vehicle from them before and know they have great customer service. Maybe it is because of the things you and your friends have experienced with them *after* the sale. The bottom line is that when you are trying to choose the right retirement vehicle for you and your family, do your homework. The vehicle you choose needs to be the perfect fit for your family, and it will need to get you where you want to go. That is not a decision to take lightly or make quickly—and certainly not just because someone bought you a steak dinner.

Listen to Someone with Skin in the Game

Earlier I mentioned Tom Hegna. Tom is a renowned international economist, best-selling author, and public speaker who talks about financial planning all over the world. He wrote the best-selling book, *Paychecks and Playchecks: Retirement Solutions for Life*, and he has worked in the retirement planning industry for over thirty years. Tom served for over twenty-two years in the US Army and US Army Reserve, retiring in 2006 as a lieutenant colonel with numerous awards and decorations. In his new book, *Don't Worry, Retire Happy!: Seven Steps to Retirement Security*, he talks about how to develop a worry-free retirement plan that will bless your family for generations. (*I highly recommend Tom's book to you if you are serious about increasing your retirement planning knowledge and want to take a good financial inventory of your own plan.*)

While writing this book, I listened to an interview with Tom, and he was talking about his "Retire Happy Now" concepts. He said something worth sharing. As we all know, 2020 was filled with UPS and DOWNS in the markets. It was like a roller coaster ride filled with major twists and turns—the kind that leaves your stomach in knots.

Tom was discussing the topic that is the title of this chapter: making sure you pick the RIGHT FINANCIAL VEHICLE for your retirement. He said there are many different options to choose from and cautioned people to be very careful to pick the ones that will work best in their situation. After using some specific examples, he said the following:

> *You have no idea how many people have interrupted my presentations to say that real estate is their "annuity." People will always need a place to stay; properties always increase in value ... yada, yada, yada. While I am not against owning real estate, it should NEVER be used to cover basic living expenses in retirement. Well, those real estate lovers are finding out why I have been saying that. Renters aren't paying rent, and landlords cannot evict them. How wonderful. ... Plus the fact that by the time people are in their 70s and 80s, all of the tax breaks have been used up, the buildings are falling apart, and those properties are now like a ball and chain around the necks of the owners. Look, we have to stick to products that are truly guaranteed. Life insurance and annuities just cannot be replaced by stocks, bonds, real estate, or Bitcoin.*[6]

Tom understands better than anyone that retirement isn't a "one-size-fits-all" concept—and that when it comes to *SAFETY* and *GUARANTEED INCOME FOR LIFE*, there are very few financial vehicles that can accomplish these pur-

---

6 Tom Hegna. Facebook, April 20, 2020.

poses and get you to your desired destination. And if you choose a vehicle that is not designed to provide safety and guaranteed income, you will end up stuck and devastated.

Tom Hegna is open about his own retirement financial plan. In fact, he very openly shares the fact that he owns eleven annuities. That is not a typo. He owns five income annuities, three fixed indexed annuities (FIAs), and three variable annuities (VAs). He goes into specific detail about why he owns so many different annuities, and he talks about the purposes for them. Oh yeah, he also owns life insurance. And a lot of it!

As I mentioned in Chapter 1, I was in Denver, Colorado, in March of 2020 with Ed Slott, who has been called "*America's IRA Expert.*" Ed was the keynote speaker for a national conference for two hundred of the nation's TOP financial advisors. We had absolutely no idea this would be the last time many of us would fly or travel in 2020. The COVID-19 pandemic was just starting to hit the news, and it was just days after the conference that all airline travel virtually came to a halt.

The day Ed spoke to the advisors, the stock market had just started a free fall. In fact, during the days surrounding the conference, the stock market dropped 257 points, 970 points, and 2,014 points. The −2,014 loss was an almost 8 percent loss in value, and it was the largest one-day loss in the stock market since the 2008 crisis. During Ed's talk, he reminded everyone that he speaks to retirees across the country. He has been the host of five different PBS shows over the years, and his 2020 PBS show was titled *Retire Safe & Secure*. So it is safe to say that Ed has his finger on the pulse of today's retirement crowd. And he reminded the group of national advisors that "today's retiree is not looking for the next hot stock or the next trendy investment idea."

He said, "The average retiree's number one purpose is to PROTECT what they have spent their entire life earning."[7] He told us that retirees don't ever want to run out of money and reminded us that his mother, who had recently passed away, spent the remainder of her years with guaranteed lifetime income that came in monthly from an annuity she owned. This money kept coming in no matter what the markets did. He said she was so proud of the fact that she had protected her money, which meant she would never be a burden on her children. Even when she was in the hospital in her last days, Ed said she would always tell him to make sure she was still getting her checks. And then he

---

7   Ed Slott, Keynote speech at the Aegis Financial "Elevate" National Conference, Denver, CO, March 4, 2021.

laughed and said he would take the cancelled checks to her and show her the money was still coming in month after month no matter what. That is what you call "*having skin in the game.*" Tom Hegna and Ed Slott are financial experts. They understand economics, taxation, and retirement planning better than most people who call themselves "advisors" or "experts." They have personally benefited from having financial plans based on owning the right retirement vehicle for themselves and their families. There is something to be said about financial planning and the *peace of mind* that comes from knowing you have established accounts that will remain SAFE and never run out of money no matter what happens in the markets.

Chapter 5: Summary and Questions

- When it comes to retirement planning, there are many different vehicles to choose from.

- It is critically important to choose the right vehicle, one that is designed to get you where you want to go.

- When it comes to retirement planning, one size does not fit all.

- You can buy a retirement vehicle from any advisor on any street corner. But what comes with that retirement vehicle and advisor should help determine where you buy it. Not all advisors are created equally.

- If your advisor suggests you buy or invest in something they do not personally own, run the other way. Ask them to show you their own retirement plan. See how they have done for themselves.

- Have you ever heard a so-called expert say, "Never buy an annuity"?

- Have you ever thought through why they said that? What is in it for them? Are they trying to sell you something else?

- How important is it to work with a Certified Financial Fiduciary®, someone who is legally bound to do what is ethical, moral, and in your best interest at all times?

- Is your current financial advisor a Certified Financial Fiduciary®? If not, why?
- Are you one hundred percent certain you have the RIGHT VEHICLES for the retirement plan of your dreams?

Chapter 6

Guaranteed Lifetime Income

"The problem with socialism is that you eventually run out of other people's money."
—*Margaret Thatcher*

Do you remember the story about my client from Chapter 1? She was within six months of retiring from a lifelong career. She had successfully saved more than $400,000 in her thrift savings plan (TSP) account at work. But when she opened her April 2020 first-quarter statement, she saw that her account value was down almost $100,000. Her $410,000 balance from January 1, 2020, had dropped to $319,932.70 on March 31, 2020, and she had made $6,164.20 in contributions during that quarter. One can only imagine how she felt.

If you were six months away from your retirement date, and you opened your retirement account statement and saw that your balance was down by 25 percent, how would it affect you? Would you panic? Would you postpone your plans for retirement? What would you do?

I can tell you what my father did. I am a second-generation financial planner. My father has been in the insurance and financial planning industry for more than fifty years. He worked for Blue Cross/Blue Shield, Merrill Lynch, and as an independent advisor representative. My father was valedictorian of his high school class and is one of the most educated people I know. He was on the dean's list as an honor student in college, and he was the commander of the ROTC Corp of Cadets at Arkansas Tech University. He is a Chartered Life Underwriter (CLU) and a Chartered Financial Consultant (ChFC). He obtained his Series 7, Series 65, and Series 63 licenses in addition to his life and health licenses. He specialized in working with company 401(k) plans and individual retirement plans throughout his career. To say he is educated would be an understatement.

However, his education did not protect his Merrill Lynch 401(k) from complete disaster when the stock market collapsed in 2001 when he was 56 years old. He was not near retirement, but he could certainly see it around the corner. After "staying the course," as most brokers tell you to do during a financial crisis, he watched his accounts slowly come back after losing nearly 50 percent. You probably know what's coming next, don't you? Just about the time he was close to recovering the losses from the 2001 market crash, the next market catastrophe came out of nowhere. Say hello to the 2008–2009 financial crisis—which took his Merrill Lynch retirement account on a roller coaster ride through dips, twists, and turns that would make any person sick to their stomach. Only, this stock market crash was much worse than the crash in 2001 because my father was now seven years older. There's a BIG difference between being a 56-year-old and being a 63-year-old when it comes to retirement planning.

Over the years, I have told thousands of people, "I know a man who can tell you how to turn a $1 million 401(k) into a $350,000 401(k)." Here is a little secret: My father is an EXPERT in finance! So how in the world does something like this happen? It happens *by having the wrong plan at the wrong time* in your life. Remember what Ed Slott says about the difference between lettuce and garbage: TIMING!

The 2001 and 2008 financial disasters were horrific for people in their fifties and sixties. They happened too close together, and there was not enough time to recover from the losses and fees before retirement. It was even worse for people in their seventies and eighties because they took distributions from their accounts while experiencing those losses and fees. That is why it is critically important to develop a *bulletproof, recession-proof,* and *pandemic-proof* retirement plan that you can trust for the rest of your life, no matter how long that may be.

The beautiful thing about the situations you just read about is that there is an alternative plan. There is a way out of the stress and the chaos of rolling the dice and hoping the stock market continues to go up throughout your retirement years. There are bulletproof financial instruments that are safe and secure, and they will provide lifetime income that will last the rest of your life. And thankfully, my father and my clients now own accounts like this, and they no longer worry about their financial future.

In 2009, while experiencing the pain of a second financial crisis in less than a decade, my father listened to what I had to say. He had been my financial advisor throughout my life, but it was time for him to learn something from the new kid on the block. I talked to him about something he had never owned in his entire financial planning career. It was called a fixed indexed annuity (FIA). When I told him about it, he quickly let me know how the brokerage side of the financial industry felt about FIAs. They would often tell clients they were the worst investment you could possibly own because they did not offer them to their clients. It is like asking the Ford guy how he feels about a Chevy. What do you think they are going to say about a product they do not offer their clients? But after having lost more than 50 percent of his retirement accounts TWICE in less than ten years, I had his attention. I asked him to consider lowering his risk corridor from 100 percent in various variable accounts to something safe and secure. After all, he was 63 years old and near retirement, and he simply could not afford to go through another 2001 or 2008.

My father decided to move some of his money from risk to safety. And he added an income rider to his account, gaining a guaranteed income stream he could never outlive. This account allowed him to link his interest to different indexes, like the S&P 500 and the Dow Jones, but his money was not invested directly in the stock market. When the markets went up, he was able to participate in the gains, and when the markets went down as they did in 2001 and again in 2008, he would keep 100 percent of his principal and his guaranteed lifetime income SAFE.

My father liked this so much that he moved the rest of the money from his Merrill Lynch 401(k) out of the stock market and into the SAFETY of two more FIAs a few years later. Now he owns three FIAs; one is a traditional IRA, and two are Roth IRAs. He is a fast learner, and he understood very quickly there is one thing that will always beat guaranteed lifetime income: guaranteed TAX-FREE lifetime income. So, he converted a significant portion of his tax-deferred money to tax-free money. He dealt with Uncle Sam on his terms and on his timetable, rather than the other way around (more on this in the next chapter). As a result, he never has to worry about the stock market. All three of his FIA retirement accounts provide guaranteed lifetime income to my mother and him, no matter how long they live. That is something that provides peace of mind in retirement.

Back to my client with the TSP. She found herself within six months of her desired retirement date with a MAJOR problem. Her account had suddenly dropped almost $100,000 and was now down by almost 25 percent. How would she retire now? Would she have to keep working, continuing to make contributions and hoping the stock market would go back up? What if she retired and the stock market took another major drop when she was no longer working and now taking distributions? What if she ran out of income? Would she have to go back to work? Every retiree faces these types of questions, which creates a lot of stress.

When we met in June of 2020, just after the 35 percent market crash, I told her something that was probably hard for her to hear. I suggested that she give it some time to see if the markets would come back. Since she had just been burned by a $96,000 drop in her account, the continued risk made her very nervous. However, the markets did come back up. In fact, they came back up in record time. There has never been a market increase after a crash that happened as quickly as the recovery in 2020. It was the fastest recovery in the history of the stock market. We took advantage of the gains in her account, and because she was older than fifty-nine and a half, she was able to take advantage of an in-service withdrawal." (See Chapter 4.)

By the time we did a TSP rollover to an IRA, her account had grown back up to $403,000. Wow, what a roller coaster ride! In less than six months, her $416,000-plus retirement account had dropped down to $319,900 and had grown back up to $403,385.80. Have you ever heard the phrase, "buy low, sell high?" The market had just hit an all-time new high. She took advantage of the gains, rolled over her money, and said GOODBYE to risk and worry for the rest of her life.

The type of FIA we used for her rollover offered a 7 percent bonus when opening the account. The **bonus** on a $403,385.80 rollover was **$28,237.01**. Her account value on day one was $431,622.81. And because of the protection this type of retirement account offers, she will keep 100 percent of her money SAFE and SECURE, protected from any future market fluctuations. Do you think she was happy? Do you think she was able to take a huge sigh of relief and get her focus back on her retirement, which was just a few months away?

While all this is great news, it is not the best part of the story. This FIA account has a special benefit and feature that anyone can add to their retirement account, and I make this available to every one of my clients. (Keep reading.)

How Long Will Your Retirement Last?

In July of 2019, I was the "Guest IRA Expert" for Ed Slott's IRA Advisor newsletter that goes out to advisors and consumers across the country. I have been the Guest IRA Expert several times over the years, but in 2019, I wrote about the main topic of this book. The article was titled, "The Stress-Free Retirement Income Plan: The Benefits of Annuities in an IRA." You can read this article on my website at www.guaranteedsafemoney.com.

In this article, I dive into some of the benefits of owning the right kind of annuity combined with an income rider. These income riders are often referred to as "lifetime income benefit riders" or "guaranteed living withdrawal benefits." Doesn't that sound wonderful? After reading this article, you will probably understand why I have written more than 1,000 annuities for my clients, and you will see why I personally now own six different FIAs in my own retirement plan. I opened my first annuity on May 2, 2008. I rolled over my 403(b) to an IRA and then immediately converted that IRA to a Roth IRA. I paid the tax due that year and got rid of Uncle Sam forever. I did not lose one penny of my retirement money during the 2008 financial crisis, and I have not lost any of my money since. I opened my sixth FIA in April of 2021. I have thirteen years of personal history with FIAs in my own financial planning, and I openly share my returns with all my clients.

As you think about your retirement accounts and future plans, let me ask you a very important question: *How long do you want your retirement to last?* It is not a trick question. Is your current plan based on <u>assumptions</u> or <u>guarantees</u>? If you experienced a steep market correction (like the ones that happened in 2001, 2008, and 2020) *during your retirement years*, would you be able to sustain your desired level of income? Would you have to change your lifestyle? Would you have to consider going back to work? Do you ever worry about running out of money before you run out of life? If so, you are not alone. It is currently the number one fear of all retirees. There is a much better way to live. Peace of mind should be the goal and desire of every retiree. Let me show you how to find it.

It does not matter if you have a 401(k), IRA, TSP, 403(b), Roth IRA, or cash sitting in the bank. You can structure your retirement accounts to give you a monthly paycheck for the rest of your life and your spouse's life if you so desire. You can also structure accounts that will provide lifetime income to any other family member you choose. You are 100 percent in control of what happens with your accounts. When it comes to retirement planning, the number one thing to establish from the very beginning is *securing guaranteed lifetime income*—which can only happen when you use the right type of account that offers guaranteed income.

When you are outside working in the yard and you turn on the water faucet, what do you expect to happen? You expect to see water, right? And you want to be in control of how quickly and how strong the water flows. You know all you need do is turn the dial one way or the other, and you will get what you want—water! You probably expect that water to continue to flow, no matter how long it takes to get the job done. That is your expectation.

The same thing is true when it comes to retirement income. When you "turn on" the income from the retirement accounts you have established, I am sure you expect the income from that account to come out immediately at your desired level and for as long as you need it. But what happens if it does not? What happens if you turn it on and then you run out of water (income)? What if your faucet (retirement account) gets water (income) from a source that is not guaranteed? What if the water pressure fluctuates? Sometimes it is good. Sometimes it is not good. Perhaps sometimes it stops altogether. What will you do?

I believe in establishing as many "water faucets" as I possibly can for my retirement plan. I want to know that no matter what is happening in the stock market or the world around me, I can walk over to any faucet at any time and turn it on, and I expect the water to flow immediately. I want to know that the source of my water (income) in each faucet is guaranteed for the rest of my life. If I want to turn on one, I can. If I need to turn on two, I can. If I want to turn them all on, I can. And I have the peace of mind that comes from knowing the water will continue to flow, no matter how bad the drought around me might be. I want it to be bulletproof, crisis-proof, and pandemic-proof. I want to know that it is safe and secure and will last the rest of my life.

One of the best features that are available with most FIAs is the income rider. When structured correctly, this income rider gives a contractual guarantee to the owner, giving them the option to receive a guaranteed lifetime income stream. I have a lifetime income benefit rider on four of my six FIAs. These "water faucets" will be used for lifetime income whenever I decide I need it. I am 100 percent in control. Once I decide to turn the faucet on and start the income, it will last for the rest of my life.

In *Don't Worry, Retire Happy!*, Tom Hegna talks about Brian Heckert and Rao Garuda. They are both financial planning professionals and colleagues. I have personally known Rao for years. He is a member of the Ed Slott Master Elite IRA Advisor group, and I see him twice a year. He is a great man and a good friend. Many years ago, he helped me develop my retirement income plan. His advice changed my life forever. I have been following his advice and plan in my personal life and in business for over a decade.

In his book, Tom refers to Brian Heckert's advice on establishing the right plan for every individual. I agree with him 100 percent. Brian (a CLU and ChFC) says, "*The most important part of retirement planning is the plan itself. Once the plan is developed, the products that fund the plan will fall into place. If income is the most important part of the plan, products like annuities that are built for income become the most important parts of the plan, and the other investments can then be built around that income base.*"[8]

In 2020, as a result of the pandemic and COVID-19, our vocabulary changed. We learned new phrases like "the new normal." In July of 2020, Dr. David Kelly wrote an interesting piece for J.P. Morgan Asset Management titled "The annuity advantage in the new economy." In this article, he explains what I have said for many years:

> *It is very difficult to estimate how long a specific sixty-five-year-old individual will live but it is very easy to estimate, on average, how long a large group of sixty-five-year-olds will live. Guaranteed income-producing annuities all leverage*

---

8 Hegna, *Don't Worry, Retire Happy!* 21.

> *this simplest of advantages: relying on the law of large numbers. This advantage means insurers are inherently able to provide higher income streams—and with higher certainty that payments will last a lifetime—than the average investor could do for him or herself. An individual has to plan for the worst. An insurer only has to plan for the average. If you are an individual turning sixty-five today, in order to be 95 percent sure that you are not going to outlive your retirement plan, you will need to generate income for thirty-three years. However, an insurance company constructing an annuity only needs to provide an income stream that lasts for twenty-one years. Twelve fewer years of payments means the payments themselves can reasonably be larger.[9]*

He goes on to say, "Unfortunately, low interest rates and high volatility in stocks indicate that retirement income planning is more challenging

---

9 Dr. David Kelly, "The Annuity Advantage in the New Economy: Part 1," The annuity advantage in the new economy: Part 1 | J.P. Morgan Asset Management (JP Morgan Chase & Co.), accessed May 27, 2021, https://am.jpmorgan.com/us/en/asset-management/adv/insights/retirement-insights/annuity-insights/the-annuity-advantage-in-the-new-economy-part-1/.

than ever. Some have called the current financial climate a 'new normal,' where economic growth will be slower and inflation lower than in decades gone by. We generally agree with this characterization, and consequently expect returns on both stocks and bonds to be substantially lower going forward. However, it turns out that in a 'new normal' economy, the benefits of annuitization are even more powerful in relative terms. In the 'new normal' economy, the benefits of annuities are even more powerful."[10]

For the record, the benefits of annuities and income riders have been extremely powerful for many years. It did not take a pandemic or a "new normal" for this to become a fact. Annuities and income riders have helped save millions of clients from absolute economic failure during their retirement years. Current economic factors have made large brokerage firms and financial advisors, who had previously focused solely on market-driven investments, take a closer look at the guarantees and benefits of annuities and income riders. And they like what they see for good reason. Guaranteed lifetime income is always in the client's best interest.

---

10 Dr. David Kelly, "The Annuity Advantage in the New Economy: Part 1."

The client I mentioned at the beginning of this book and in this chapter now has peace of mind. She recovered her losses, protected her principal, and secured her guaranteed lifetime income stream, *the most important part of any retirement plan.* She watched her account drop more than $96,000 in a matter of months, but now her account is higher than it has ever been, and it is SAFE and SECURE. She has a *lifetime income benefit rider* attached to her retirement account, guaranteeing her a lifetime income stream she can never outlive. In February of 2021, she stepped out of the working world into the world of retirement, just like she had planned. She turned the water faucet on, and the water will continue to come out for the rest of her life, no matter what happens in the stock market or the world around her. She is now able to live the retirement of her dreams. What an incredible feeling!

Chapter 6: Summary and Questions

- The 2001 and 2008 financial crises ruined the retirement plans of millions of people. They did not realize their plan had problems until the crisis hit.

- If you are retired and taking distributions from your retirement accounts during a financial downturn, you face the risk of complete financial disaster if your accounts do not provide principal protection and guaranteed lifetime income.

- Certain types of retirement accounts and products can take the guesswork out of retirement.

- Guaranteed income is ALWAYS better than hypothetical income.

- Have you ever really calculated your financial longevity?

- *Do you know how long your financial assets will last based on your current plan?*

- Are you 100 percent certain your current financial plan will provide guaranteed lifetime income to you and your spouse, no matter what happens in the financial markets?

- Would you like to know if you are headed in the right direction?

Chapter 7

Guaranteed "Tax-Free" Lifetime Income (Even Better)

"The difference between death and taxes is death doesn't get worse every time Congress meets."

—*Will Rogers*

For just a minute, I want to talk about something I know absolutely *nothing* about. This world is filled with people who spend a lot of time talking about things they know little to nothing about, and they do so by proximity.

I have been driving a four-wheel-drive truck since I was eighteen years old. I drive a lot. Over the years, I have owned multiple farms in three different states. And like many of you, I am in my office forty to fifty hours a week, Monday–Friday. I spend a lot of time driving on the weekends. Now you would think that since I have owned four-wheel-drive trucks for more than thirty years, that I would probably know a lot about them. But I do not! Even though I am behind the wheel of a four-wheel-drive truck every single day, I know very little about what's under the hood. I know little about what makes that truck do what it's designed to do. I can change a dead battery. I can refill the window washer fluid. I can change a flat tire. Outside of that—NOTHING, NADA, ZERO! If something happens to my truck and it stops running the way it is supposed to, I take it straight to the *SPECIALIST* who knows exactly what to do to make it run and function at its best.

I could lift the hood and stare at the engine and act like I know what I am doing; I do not. Have you met anyone who acts as though they know what they're talking about when they do not? They might act like they are a *TRAINED SPECIALIST*. They might even have some fancy title that suggests they know more than the average person about a specific topic, but when it comes down to it, they do not! They might not know DIDLY SQUAT about the topic they are pretending to specialize in. This person could even be a senator, a congressman, or the speaker of the house.

How Much Money Is $1.9 TRILLION?

It is a serious question, and the answer is very important to your future. Why? Because our government just approved a $1.9 trillion stimulus package, and they are discussing spending trillions more on infrastructure. To help you understand just how much money $1.9 trillion is, consider this:

If one dollar equals one second, $1 million would be about eleven and a half days. And $1 BILLION would be thirty-two years, so $1 TRILLION would be 32,000 YEARS. Do you see the problem here? Now let me repeat that so you can let that sink in for a minute. If one dollar equals one second, $1 million would be about eleven and a half days. And $1 BILLION would be thirty-two years, so $1 TRILLION would be 32,000 YEARS. Again, do you see the problem here?

Our federal government is spending money like it grows on every tree on the planet, but guess what? It does not! They try to act like they are SPECIALISTS when it comes to money and finance. Hint: they are not. (*Have you seen our national debt?*). They are politicians. PERIOD!

If one dollar equals one second, and $1 TRILLION dollars equals 32,000 years, can you even begin to fathom what spending several trillion tax-payer dollars will do to your tax-deferred retirement accounts?

Let me try to explain this in a different way:

- One million is one-thousand thousands.
- One billion is one-thousand millions.
- One trillion is one-thousand billions (or, in other words, one-million millions).

If you took one million pennies and stacked them on top of each other, it would make a tower nearly a mile high. One billion pennies stacked on top of each other would make a tower almost 870 miles high. One trillion pennies stacked on top of each other would make a tower about 870,000 miles high—which would be roughly the same distance obtained by going to the moon, back to Earth, and then to the moon again.

If that does not help you visualize a trillion, maybe this last example will get your attention:

- If you earn $45,000 a year, it will take you 22 years to save $1 million.
- If you earn $45,000 a year, it will take you 22,000 years to save a billion dollars.
- If you earn $45,000 a year, it will take you 22,000,000 years to save a trillion dollars.

And keep in mind, that is only if you DIDN'T HAVE TO PAY UNCLE SAM ANY TAXES. But guess what, you do have to pay Uncle Sam. And you pay him substantial amounts of TAX! If you think these taxes will go down during your retirement because you are no longer earning your salary or income, think again.

You should take the time to google "taxation on Social Security in retirement." It will give you an education on how withdrawals from your tax-deferred 401(k), 403(b), TSP, or IRAs will affect the taxes you pay on your Social Security. Did you know this also affects the amount you will pay each year for your Medicare premiums? That is right. The majority of retirees I work with find out they pay more in taxes in retirement than they did when they were working. And they all say the same thing: "Why didn't my advisor tell me this years ago! I would have come up with a different plan!"

How many of you have been told by your CPA or your financial advisor *to take advantage of making tax-deductible contributions to your 401(k) or IRA now because your taxes will likely go DOWN once you retire*? I know the answer to that question. I have been on the radio for more than a decade, and I've talked to thousands and thousands of retirees. Very few CPAs and advisors are forward-thinking planners. As Ed Slott often says, "CPAs are history teachers. They talk to us about what just happened in the previous year." And most advisors' sole focus is on the amount of "return percent" they can get you. Do not ever forget; it is not what you MAKE; it's what you <u>KEEP</u> that counts. As I write this book, our national debt is $28 TRILLION and counting, and our government is adding TRILLIONS to this total on a regular basis!

Hopefully, this will help you understand on a deeper level. Just go to www.usdebtclock.org. On this site, you will see the current US national debt, US total debt, and the US unfunded liabilities. In addition, you will see student loan debt and what that average is per student, total personal debt and what the average is per citizen, and credit card debt totals.

You will also see how many retirees there are in the United States and how many are enrolled in Medicare and Medicaid. It will show you how many people are on food stamps, how many people live without insurance, and how many people live in poverty. It will show you how many people have filed for bankruptcy and how many people have had their homes foreclosed on. By contrast, it will also show you how many millionaires there are in the United States.

But what I would really like for you to do is pay attention to the box at the top left of the page as well as a box at the bottom right of the page. In the box at the top left, you will first see the current US national debt. But near the bottom of that box, you will find something that reads "US FEDERAL DEBT to GDP RATIO." And this should get your attention.

- In 1960, the US federal debt to GDP ratio was 53.18 percent.
- Twenty years later, in 1980, the US federal debt to GDP ratio was 34.53 percent.
- By 2000, the US federal debt to GDP had grown back to 58.96 percent.
- And currently, in 2021, the US federal debt to GDP is 129.52 percent.

Let that sink in for a minute as you think about the *future taxation* of your tax-deferred retirement accounts.

Near the bottom right of the page, you will see the following:

- Social Security Liabilities: $23 trillion
- Medicare Liabilities: $32 trillion
- US Unfunded Liabilities: $159 trillion

And finally, you will see a box that reads "Liability Per Citizen: $483,000." Do I have your attention yet?

> **"The hardest thing to understand in the world is the income tax."**
> —*Albert Einstein*

In my professional opinion, when it comes to you being able to experience the retirement of your dreams, tax planning must be near the top of your list of priorities. So, what is better than a *safe and secure retirement income plan*? A TAX-FREE, *safe and secure retirement income plan*.

One of my favorite authors and speakers is Jim Rohn. He would often say something like, "If you don't have a plan for your future and your retirement, the government will. And guess what they have planned for you? Not much!" I certainly agree with that from one perspective, but I would like to add to it. When it comes to taxes, the government has BIG plans for you. They hope you and your advisor have absolutely no idea how to maximize your tax-free retirement plans. Because if you don't, they will take control. And your family will lose the majority of what you have worked so hard to save.

When you decide to contribute to a tax-deferred account, you are not avoiding the tax. You are postponing it. You are taking a major gamble. Whether you realize it or not, you are staking your bet on the fact that taxes will be lower in the future than they are right now. You take a tax deduction now and agree to pay Uncle Sam in the future (at whatever rate he says you will owe him at that time). You either pay the tax now or you pay it later. You know the tax rate now, but you have no idea what it will be in the future. Do you see the dilemma?

I own several Roth IRAs. I also own ten life insurance policies. I own life insurance policies on my parents, my children, and myself. Why do I own multiple Roth IRAs and ten life insurance policies? Simple: TAXES!

Let's do a quick comparison of the differences between a traditional IRA and a Roth IRA.

Features, Advantages, and Benefits	Traditional IRA	Roth IRA
Required Minimum Distributions (RMDs)	YES	NO
Tax-Free Income	NO	YES
Tax Liability on Social Security Income	YES	NO
Tax-Free Growth	NO	YES
Tax-Free Transfer to Beneficiaries	NO	YES

In the preceding table, a traditional IRA could be replaced above with the following: *401(k), 403(b), TSP, and any other tax-deferred plan.* The old saying is true. Two things are absolutely certain in life: death and taxes. But, for many people, it is much worse than they think. And for many, death will trigger even MORE taxes.

Depending on the value of assets you leave to your family and the type of accounts those assets are held in, not only will you pay taxes throughout your lifetime, but your heirs might also be forced to pay the "death tax" when you die.

One of the most important things you can do for yourself and your family is work with a qualified advisor who will help you establish a safe and secure TAX PLAN for your retirement. If you do not have a plan for the taxes within your retirement plan, Uncle Sam does. He will tax your retirement accounts for generations. He will tax your spouse and your children on the accounts you will pass on to them. He will tell them how much they will have to pay, and it will make you roll over in your grave. Do not let this happen to you or those you love most.

Make the decision to do what 99 percent of all people put off doing (and regret later in life). Define your goals. Consider your family and your plans for retirement. Then choose the right financial tools that will help you accomplish those goals and those dreams. Your financial worries should retire when you do. Anyone can own stocks, bonds, mutual funds, and various investments. But very few people take the time to develop a plan designed to complement their goals and lifestyles. Even fewer people take the time to learn how to get rid of Uncle Sam NOW so that he is left 100 percent ON THE BENCH during their retirement. Just like I talk about in Chapter 8 of my No. 1 best-selling book, *Safe Money Matters: Finding Safe Harbor in a Storm-Filled World*, tax-free beats taxable every time!

As I talked about in Chapter 6, you can get the same benefits and features of the retirement accounts that are guaranteed for life, and you can structure them to pay out to you TAX-FREE for the rest of your life. That is true peace of mind planning. It will let you sleep at night. You will never have to worry about you or your spouse running out of money, no matter how long you live. And you will never have to deal with Uncle Sam's constant moving of the goalposts. (Watch my interview with Ed Slott regarding the Secure Act and TAXES at www.guaranteedsafemoney.com or on YouTube at https://www.youtube.com/watch?v=XRnUK3N9zms.)

Chapter 7: Summary and Questions

- Failing to plan is planning to fail.
- If you do not come up with a plan for your taxes, Uncle Sam will (and you will not like his plan).
- Making tax-deductible contributions to a tax-deferred account is not "saving" the tax; it is delaying it until a future date.
- You can either get rid of Uncle Sam on your terms or be forced to play by his rules.
- Have you ever calculated the benefits of getting rid of the taxes inside your retirement accounts now versus dealing with them in the future? If not, why?
- Do you know how long your financial assets will last you based on your current financial plan?
- Do you have confidence that your current financial plan will maintain your desired lifestyle for the rest of your life, no matter how long you live? Including the TAXES involved?
- Would you like to know with 100 percent certainty that you have a bulletproof plan in place for you and your family?

Chapter 8

Pursuing What Matters Most

"Let us more and more insist on raising funds of love, of kindness, of understanding, of peace. Money will come if we seek first the Kingdom of God; the rest will be given."

—*Mother Teresa*

I am sure all of you can remember a day in your life when everything seemed to change in an instant. It might have been the day you got married, the day you had your first child, or some other special event. These life-changing experiences can result from good things; they can also be the result of difficult things. For example, the day you might remember more than any other day in your life might include a diagnosis from a doctor, or it may be the day you lost your parents or a spouse. One thing is for certain: When things like these happen, the world seems to move at a much slower pace, and everything that really matters seems to stare you right in the face.

At the beginning of this book, you read about a life-changing series of events that took place in my life. On April 2, 1999, my world was brought to a screeching halt when I woke up and found myself lying in a hospital bed in the ER. When doctors found a very large tumor in my brain and recommended I see a specialist because they did not have the expertise to deal with my tumor, I was in shock. Why would a twenty-seven-year-old former college athlete have a brain tumor? It could not be true, but just a few days later, I found out how true it was. On April 15, 1999—a tax deadline day I will never forget—I endured a ten-hour surgery, and the tumor was successfully removed from my brain. Days later, I walked out of the hospital with sixty-five metal staples in my head, a completely closed left eye, and a headache like you would not believe. When people look at my post-op pictures from 1999 and see me now, it is hard for them to believe that it is was me. It is my story; I am a brain-tumor survivor. By the grace of God, I have been 100 percent tumor free since then.

The Day That Changed My Life Forever

There are several days in my life I can point to and say, "That is a day that changed my life forever." April 2 and April 15, 1999, certainly qualify. However, there is a day that stands out in the forefront of my mind, more than the day I had brain surgery.

On January 13, 2021, I came to the office expecting a normal business day. I had several clients booked with meetings to discuss their plans for retirement. Instead, about fifteen minutes before the first appointment, my son-in-law called my cell phone. I could hear my daughter crying in the background. She was due with their first child, which would be my first grandchild. But because of COVID-19, no family members were allowed at the hospital for the birth.

My son-in-law, who has a very severe, chronic headache condition, said, "Dad, I'm not doing so well. We need you." Because of the pandemic, the nurses were worried that he might have COVID-19, so they asked him to leave the room. In the blink of an eye, I ran into the front office, telling my son Hunter and our office manager Lisa, "I'm headed north. Autumn is in labor, and

Ethan is sick." When both of them told me they didn't believe I would be allowed into the hospital, I said, "You know me. What do you think the chances are that I get into that hospital this morning?" And off I went.

Two hours later, I was standing in front of the woman who would approve whether I could get past the front desk at the hospital. The list of those who qualified for entrance was very short. Every hall was blocked off, and there was only one way in and one way out. I explained that my daughter was in labor, giving birth to her first child and my first grandchild and that her husband was sick. She picked up the phone, called back to labor and delivery, and just a few minutes later, I was holding my daughter's hand and saying, "You can do this, Autumn. You were made for this. Now when I say push, PUSH. One, two, three—PUSH! Come on Autumn, PUSH. Take a deep breath and PUSH! You're doing great, Autumn, one more big push, One, two, three—PUSH." If you have ever been there, you know what an amazing, life-changing experience it is. I continued to coach Autumn for the next two hours. I repeated the same thing over and over again, "You can do this Autumn, 1-2-3 PUSH. Push, Push, PUSH!"

About ninety minutes into pushing, Autumn's doctor walked in for the first time. He took one look at me and realized I was not Autumn's husband. I introduced myself in between contractions. In just a few short minutes between my daughter's contractions, the doctor and I discovered we went to college in the same state and were in the same athletic conference. He played college football, and I played college golf. We knew some of the same people. In fact, he went to Medical School at the University of Arkansas for Medical Sciences.

When he said that, I asked, "When were you in school there?" And when he told me, I responded with, "Did you know Dr. Al-Mefty."

He replied, "Of course, he was one of the best brain surgeons in the world."

I told him, "Dr. Al-Mefty performed my brain surgery in 1999 while you were there in medical school." At one point, I noticed the doctor was talking to a nurse and had tears in his eyes.

He turned to me and said, "I'm sorry. This does not normally happen to me. I have five children. My oldest daughter is eighteen. And I am deeply touched by your relationship with your daughter."

A few minutes later, my daughter gave birth to August James Tyler Newman, a beautiful, healthy, six-pound, thirteen-ounce baby boy! They placed little Auggie in my daughter's arms, and the doctor turned to me and said, "Would you like to cut the cord?"

I have experienced a lot of life-changing moments in my fifty years on this earth. I am a very blessed man. I was honored to baptize both my son and my daughter, I performed both of their weddings, and I helped deliver my daughter's first child (my first grandchild). I even cut the cord! How many fathers in the history of the world can say that? January 13, 2021, was a *life-changing* day! It is one of those moments that will stand still in time for me, one that helps bring clarity and focus to everything else in life! I am now a PAW-PAW!

I have often heard those older than me say things like, "There's nothing quite like being a grandparent." I am sure you have, too. They also say things like, "I love my children, but having grandchildren is a completely different joy. It is special! And you just can't describe it. You'll see one day!"

And guess what? Now I see. There is simply nothing else in the world like holding my grandson and seeing him smile back at me. And when he starts laughing, the heavens open, and the sky spills over into the earth for a few wonderful minutes. January 13, 2021, is a day that changed my life forever. I will never be the same.

Do you have children? Do you have grandchildren? Do you remember what it was like the first time you saw them and held them in your arms? How did it impact your life?

Do you think my plans for retirement and for taking care of my family came into clearer focus the day my first grandchild was born? You better believe it did. Do you think I am interested in playing "games of chance" with the money that will be used to provide for my children and grandchildren for the rest of their lives? Do you think I am interested in rolling the dice and hoping the stock market will be moving in the right direction when my grandchildren go to college? ABSOLUTELY NOT! When my life on this earth comes to an end, and the good Lord calls me home, do you think I want anything that I leave to my family based on "hypothetical projections"? Or do you think I want to know beyond the shadow of a doubt that I have protected 100 percent of my assets with guarantees and that I have secured lifetime income for everyone I love? I think you know the answer. I am quite certain it is the same peace of mind planning you want to do for your family!

Legacy Planning That Lasts FOREVER

A truly stress-free retirement takes place when you never have to worry about running out of money before you run out of life. You will sleep well at night when you know your income will not only last the rest of your life and your spouse's life but also for the lives of everyone you plan to leave a legacy. That is true peace. But I like to take it a step further than that.

I recently read something that I have since passed on to many clients and friends. It even found its way onto the pages of this book. The article, "Christian Leaders Transforming the World of Wealth Management: A look into faith-fueled finance," included a section about living a legacy. Darryl Lyons, co-founder and CEO of PAX Financial Group, said, "Inheritance is what you leave to someone, but legacy is what you leave in someone. Living a legacy is much more rewarding, and much more fun, than just accumulating money to leave behind."[11]

---

11 Fralin, Jessica. "Christian Leaders Transforming the World of Wealth Management." CT Creative Studio. Christianity Today, September 21, 2020. https://www.christianitytoday.com/partners/c12/faith-fueled-finance.html.

His words are beautifully powerful and reminded me of a couple of interviews I did back in 2018 and 2019 with Robert Powell, CFP and writer for *USA Today*, The Street, Retirement Daily, and MarketWatch. Various parts of my interviews with Robert ended up in *USA Today* in the article "Why you need to have purpose in your daily life even when you retire" and in the Retirement Daily article, "What New Opportunities Are You Retiring To?"

Robert interviewed several financial advisors from across the country and pieced together their thoughts on avoiding a "let down" after retiring. He says, "It's not about retiring from work; it's about retiring to new opportunities."[12]

While Robert and I talked, I shared with him some of the research I had done regarding the high percentage of people who return to work within less than a year of retiring. There are a lot of reasons this happens, but one of the main ones is that a person's career often provides a great sense of self-worth. If you do not have a plan when you retire, then you will not retire TO something, and you will most likely feel like there is no reason to get up each day. In fact, one of the most important things you can do once you retire is to actively

---

12 Powell, Robert, "What New Opportunities Are You Retiring To?" January 22, 2019. https://www.thestreet.com/retirement-daily/.

participate in the lives of your children and grandchildren. Do the things you always wished you could do but never could because you were working. Volunteer to coach a grandchild's sports team or volunteer at church or a civic organization. Use your talents to volunteer for a worthy cause and continue to make a difference in the lives of the people you are serving.

The key is to retire TO something rather than FROM something. Most people spend their entire adult lives giving their time and using their talents for their careers. And for some reason, this comes to an abrupt stop the day they retire, which creates an incredible sense of loss. Your desire to create, help other people, and use your talents and abilities does not go on permanent vacation the day you retire. If you do not put them to use daily, you will lose your sense of purpose and experience a great sense of loss. For the first time in your life, you do not have to say, "If I only had the time, I would . . . " You have the time to do whatever you want to do, and you should do exactly that.

Do not forget; you have worked hard. You have spent your entire adult life preparing for this very special time of life. Hopefully, you have assembled your team of experts and specialists and come up with a *Bulletproof, Safe and Secure Retirement Income Plan* that will last the rest of your life! That provides an incredible, peaceful feeling. But your journey is only beginning. Now the FUN part of life begins. You are no longer punching a clock. There are no deadlines to meet. Instead, you get to wake up every morning and CHANGE LIVES. What a beautiful thing!

So do whatever you want to do. Take that vacation and bring your grandchildren along. Go on a mission trip and teach your grandchildren what life is about. Coach a basketball team and watch young lives change because you took the time to care. Find your passion. Use your talents. Give your time. Serve other people. Teach a child to fish or hunt. Take them camping. Build fires. Stare at the stars. Tell stories (always tell stories).

You will find out that TRUE RICHES will pour into your life when you GIVE BACK to those around you. Leaving a true legacy is more about *how you live* and *how you give*. It is not what you leave to someone; it is what you leave in them that matters the most! Give the best gift you could ever give them: *your time*! They will never be the same, and you will live the retirement of your dreams! The memories you make will lead to the stories they will share with their children and grandchildren for decades to come. That is legacy planning that truly lasts forever.

Auggie's first trip to see Paw-Paw at his office

Chapter 8: Summary and Questions

- Some days and events change our lives forever. These events give us perspective.

- Make sure you have a retirement plan in place. Instead of retiring FROM something, retire TO something.

- Your children and grandchildren won't remember how much money you gave TO them; they will remember the legacy you leave IN them.

- Do you remember a day that changed your life forever? Why is it unforgettable?

- How did this event change you or your perspective on life?

- What do you plan to retire TO?

- What do you plan to leave IN the people you love the most?

- Have you taken the time to develop your *Bulletproof, Safe and Secure Retirement Income Plan* so you can live the retirement of your dreams and leave behind a legacy that will last forever?

- If not, why?

Choosing the Right Financial Team

"Retirement Money is one of your largest assets. Are you working with the right advisor?"

Your hard-earned money is at high risk of being lost to taxes and fees if your advisor does not know to ask you the right questions, isn't aware of changes to the turbulent tax code, and/or hasn't been trained in high-level retirement planning strategies.

Are you making the right moves with your retirement, or are you building a savings account for Uncle Sam? The answer lies in education and working with a qualified advisor.

Members of Ed Slott's Elite IRA Advisor Group℠ train with Ed Slott and Company on a continual basis, have completed requisite training, passed a background check, attended required workshops, and completed mandatory exams. They are immediately notified of changes to the tax code and updates on retirement planning, so you can be sure your retirement dollars are safe from unnecessary taxes and fees.

Retirement planning is complicated, and you need an IRA specialist in this area. It is a personal and situational endeavor with possible pitfalls in the way of success. Work with a financial professional who invests in his/her education to eliminate risk and keep more of your retirement dollars for you and your family.

With new tax laws, important IRS rulings, and an ever-changing financial climate, it is more important than ever for advisors to continually invest in their education. Members of Ed Slott's Elite IRA Advisor Group℠ are dedicated to being leaders in the IRA industry and protecting their clients' families' futures.

—Ed Slott, *America's IRA Expert*

> To find a qualified advisor in your area, please visit:
> https://www.irahelp.com/find-an-advisor

Brad Pistole, Rao Garuda, and Ed Slott

About Ed Slott, CPA

Ed Slott, CPA, America's IRA Expert, is a nationally recognized speaker, television personality, and best-selling author known for his unparalleled ability to turn advanced tax strategies into understandable, actionable, and entertaining advice.

Named "The Best Source for IRA Advice" by the *Wall Street Journal,* he is the go-to resource for media, regularly providing insight on breaking news affecting retirement and tax planning laws and strategies.

Mr. Slott is a Professor of Practice at The American College of Financial Services and has been recognized by leading industry organizations for his significant thought leadership and contributions. He is one of the top pledge drivers of all time with his popular public television specials, the creator of Ed Slott's Elite IRA Advisor Group℠, and most recently published *The New Retirement Savings Time Bomb: How to Take Financial Control, Avoid Unnecessary Taxes, and Combat the Latest Threats to Your Retirement Savings* (2021). Ultimately, through all of these efforts combined, Mr. Slott has taught millions of Americans (and their financial professionals) how to get the most out of their retirement savings.

Suggested Reading

- *The New Retirement Savings Time Bomb: How to Take Financial Control, Avoid Unnecessary Taxes, and Combat the Latest Threats to Your Retirement Savings* by Ed Slott, CPA
- *Stay Rich for Life!: Growing & Protecting Your Money in Turbulent Times* by Ed Slott, CPA
- *Don't Worry, Retire Happy!: Seven Steps to Retirement Security* by Tom Hegna
- *Stress-Free Retirement* by Patrick Kelly
- *The Retirement Miracle* by Patrick Kelly
- *The Power of Zero: How to Get to the 0% Tax Bracket and Transform Your Retirement* by David McKnight
- *Money. Wealth. Life Insurance.: How the Wealthy Use Life Insurance as a Tax-Free Personal Bank to Supercharge Their Savings* by Jake Thompson
- *Safe Money Matters: Finding Safe Harbor in a Storm-Filled World* by Brad Pistole

FOR IMMEDIATE RELEASE:

Contact:

Brad Pistole

Phone: **(417) 581-9222**

Email: brad@guaranteedsafemoney.com

Institute of Business & Finance Announces a New CAS® Designee

San Diego, CA, June 15, 2020 — The Institute of Business & Finance (IBF) recently awarded **Brad Pistole** with the only nationally recognized annuity designation, **CAS® (Certified Annuity Specialist®).** This graduate-level designation is conferred upon candidates who complete a 135+ hour educational program focusing on fixed-rate and variable annuities. Several trillion dollars are invested in annuities; it is estimated that at least one-third of all annuity contracts are not titled correctly.

CAS® certification requires mastery of contract structure, tax ramifications, strategies, income structuring, equity-indexed products, and principals of asset allocation. According to IBF, "Annuities can provide the cornerstone of an effective financial or estate plan. The practitioner and client need to understand when such an investment vehicle is appropriate and when it should be avoided."

The student must pass three comprehensive exams, complete a written case study as well as adhere to the *IBF Code of Ethics* and *IBF Standards of Practice* as well as fulfill annual continuing education requirements. **The CAS® program is designed for brokers and advisors who have clients seeking estate preservation protection, an income stream they cannot outlive, tax benefits, or the upside potential of the stock market without any downside risk.**

ABOUT THE INSTITUTE OF BUSINESS & FINANCE — Founded in 1988, IBF is a nonprofit provider of financial education and designations to members of the financial services industry. IBF is the fourth oldest provider of financial certification marks in the United States. In 1988, IBF launched its first certification program, CFS® (Certified Fund Specialist®). Today, IBF offers four additional financial designation programs: CAS® (Certified Annuity Specialist®), CES™ (Certified Estate and Trust Specialist™), CIS™ (Certified Income Specialist™) and CTS™ (Certified Tax Specialist™).

-END-

State Rep. Lynn Morris recognizes Brad Pistole with the Missouri House of Representatives Resolution for outstanding achievements in the financial industry on January 19, 2019.

About the Author

Brad Pistole, Certified Financial Fiduciary® and Certified Annuity Specialist®, graduated with a Bachelor of Science in Education from Arkansas Tech University in 1993. He holds life, health, and property & casualty licenses in Missouri, Arkansas, Kansas, Oklahoma, and Texas. Brad specializes in several different aspects of financial planning, including retirement income planning, 401(k) and IRA rollovers, Roth IRA conversions, and tax-free retirement through special types of life insurance. He shows his clients how to use accounts that will reduce, defer, or even eliminate their taxes. These accounts have no risk of principal loss, and they provide a lifetime of income the clients will never outlive.

Because of his expertise in retirement planning, Brad has been recognized nationally as a member of the Ed Slott Master Elite IRA Advisor Group since 2010. His professional affiliations include the National Ethics Association and the Million Dollar Round Table (MDRT). As a member of the MDRT's Top of the Table, he ranks among the top 1 percent of that prestigious organization. As a Certified Financial Fiduciary®, Brad has taken an oath to do what is in the best interest of his clients at all times.

A gifted writer and speaker, Brad has shared his financial expertise through books, articles, and speaking engagements. In addition, he is the weekly host of *Safe Money Radio*, airing in Missouri and Arkansas on several different stations. In 2018, he was recognized as the *Safe Money Radio* National Advisor of the Year. **In 2019, Brad was recognized with the Missouri House of Representatives Resolution from state Rep. Lynn Morris for outstanding achievements in the financial industry.** He is also very involved in mentoring and helping financial advisors all across the country. You can reach Brad by phone at 417-581-9222 or via email at brad@guaranteedsafemoney.com. Learn more about Brad at https://www.guaranteedsafemoney.com/media.html.

When Brad is not at the office, he loves to spend time at his farms with his best buddy, "Patch." He and Patch love to hunt, fish, and enjoy the outdoors. Brad is an early-to-bed/early-to-rise person who knows some of life's greatest lessons are learned before the sun ever comes up. He believes watching the sunrise and sunset from the back porch with those you love is the best part of every day. Brad says the best books and radio shows in the world are written in one's mind while on a tractor in the middle of God's creation!

He was a full-time youth and family life minister from 1991–2007 and is currently involved with two different ministries. Brad provides financial and spiritual support to a local pastor (The Way Church in Webb City, Missouri) and a missionary and his family who live in Honduras (Breaking Chains Honduras (bchonduras.org).

Brad has two children, Autumn and Hunter, and was blessed to baptize them and perform each of their wedding ceremonies. He became a Paw-Paw in 2021 and spends as much time as possible with "little Auggie." Brad wants to remind everyone that legacy is not what you leave TO someone; it's what you leave IN someone that lasts forever. Psalm 37:3-5, NLT.

Paw-Paw and Auggie at the *Safe Money Radio* studios

Brad and Patch at the office

Sunrise at the farm

About the Author

Brad and Patch